THE SOCIAL DETERMINATION OF KNOWLEDGE

JUDITH WILLER

Prentice-Hall, Inc., Englewood Cliffs, New Jersey

©1971 by Prentice-Hall, Inc., Englewood Cliffs, New Jersey

Prentice-Hall General Sociology Series
Neil J. Smelser, Editor

13–815563–1

Library of Congress Card Catalog Number: 72–143580

Printed in the United States of America

Current Printing (Last Digit):

10   9   8   7   6   5   4   3   2   1

PRENTICE-HALL INTERNATIONAL, INC., *London*
PRENTICE-HALL OF AUSTRALIA, PTY. LTD., *Sydney*
PRENTICE-HALL OF CANADA, LTD., *Toronto*
PRENTICE-HALL OF INDIA PRIVATE LIMITED, *New Delhi*
PRENTICE-HALL OF JAPAN, INC., *Tokyo*

To my father and mother, Darrel and Janet Abel

CONTENTS

v

PREFACE

The study of knowledge is a broad area usually separated into smaller pieces such as the philosophy of science and the sociology of religion. This book considers four types of knowledge (magic, mysticism, religion, and science) from one point of view. By conceptualizing types of knowledge as systems made up of particular ways of thinking and notions of power, these four types may be understood more clearly because they are unified in a theoretical scheme and, at the same time, they are clearly separated according to specific criteria.

Primitive beliefs are often confused with less primitive ones, religion in modern civilization is frequently separated from more primitive beliefs only by its wider scope, and scientific knowledge is sometimes attributed to any group which practices careful observation. The purpose of this book is to point out that distinct types of knowledge and associated actions can be theoretically isolated, and that magic, mysticism, religion, and science make characteristic appearances in certain social situations. Each of these theoretical types of knowledge is viewed in its empirical environment from primitive society to the complex structures of the modern world; but, although the types vary in complexity, this attribute alone does not determine their predominant existence in any social structure. The theory presented here is theoretically determinative but not evolutionary.

I would like to thank Robert Bierstedt, Ernest Mannheim, and Murray Wax for their help and suggestions, Richard Cole for his continued encouragement, and especially my husband, David Willer, for his patience, intellectual stimulation, and sacrifice of his own valuable time enabling me to complete my work.

INTRODUCTION

One of the most intricate and profound of all of the sectors of sociology is the sociology of knowledge. It is a sector in which serious and complex questions are raised about the nature of knowledge itself. These questions are not narrowly epistemological in the traditional sense but more broadly sociological. They concern the social determinants and consequences of knowledge.

This kind of inquiry can be approached from various directions. One of them, favored by Florian Znaniecki and treated with both literary and sociological distinction in his book *The Social Role of the Man of Knowledge*, has to do with those who occupy themselves with knowledge in various societies—priests, sages, scholars, technologists, scientists, and "explorers," the last meaning that small number of thinkers in any society who are discoverers and innovators, those who create new knowledge. It has to do with the ways in which societies define and support the roles these thinkers play and with the ways also in which the roles fit into the social structure and attract a differential prestige. It has to do in addition with the social organization of the production of knowledge. Does the scientist work best alone or is there some advantage in being a member of a group? How is scientific research sustained and subsidized? What is the relationship between science and government? What are the social responsibilities of scientists and how do they respond to the anguished cry of Saint-Simon, who reprimanded them in 1813: "All Europe is in a death-struggle. What are you doing to stop this butchery? Nothing. It is you who perfect the means of destruction."

A second direction, quite different, leads to logical rather than ethical speculation. It is along this road that logic, sociology, and epistemology meet in a kind of modern trivium. The problem here is the social base and foundation of knowledge or, as Judith Willer expresses it as the title of her book, "the social determination of knowledge."

When we were first introduced to philosophy we were taught that the origin of a belief has nothing to do with its truth; that is, if the premises are acceptable and the process of reasoning is valid, then the conclusion too is acceptable or at least, in the language of John Dewey, that we are warranted in asserting it. The warranted assertibility of a proposition—we were required to believe—has nothing to do with the person who asserts it and cannot possibly be affected by his age, sex, religion, nationality, state of health, or attributes of personality. All such variables are irrelevant to its truth. To think otherwise is to commit, at the very least, the fallacy of *argumentum ad hominem.*

The matter, however, may not be so simple. There may be something not about the individual but about society that influences the nature of knowledge. Is it possible, for example, that questions that demand answers in one society, at one period of history, are not even asked in another society, at another period? Here one would clearly respond in the affirmative. No one in modern industrial societies wonders whether, if God is all-powerful, he can restore virginity to a prostitute; no one debates whether the mouse that steals into the cathedral and eats the consecrated wafer has partaken of the body of Christ; and no one asks himself why God, who is presumed to be eternal, did not create the universe, say, some 600,000 years earlier than he did. (What was he waiting for?) Similarly, no one in tenth century Europe wondered whether the speed of light is a constant, whether the structure of DNA, the heredity molecule, is singly or doubly helical, or whether the division of labor in an organized group is a simple or complex function of its size.

In this direction, however, we may probe even more deeply. Is it possible that propositions that may seem to contradict one another in one society may be accepted as consistent in another? Is it possible that the canons of logic in terms of which we judge propositions to be true are themselves susceptible to social determination? Is it possible that what is regarded as evidence is itself a variable and not a constant in human societies? Even the category of causation may have a different meaning and emphasis in different societies. Of Aristotle's four causes, for example, the mind of medieval man affixed itself upon the formal and the final whereas we today tend to stress the material and the efficient.

If we accept such consequences as these, of course, we are immediately set adrift upon a sea of paradox, deprived of navigational aids and of all reference points. Like Archimedes, we have no place to stand. For it must then be apparent that any proposition we might wish to assert about the sociology of knowledge is itself a victim of shifting social tides. We unhappily confront a situation in which knowledge has lost its truth and so also have all propositions in the sociology of knowledge. The ultimate and unresolvable paradox—the paradox with which Bertrand Russell wrestled so valiantly in the Introduction to *Principia Mathematica*—is that the sociology of knowledge destroys the possibility of a sociology of knowledge. In this situation we can only throw up our hands and quote, with gratitude, the immortal first sentence to the Preface of the first edition of *The Critique of Pure Reason:* "Human reason has this peculiar fate that in one species of its knowledge it is burdened by questions which, as prescribed by the very nature of reason itself, it is not able to ignore, but which, as transcending all of its powers, it is also not able to answer."

Fortunately, not all of the problems in the sociology of knowledge have this degree of complexity. It is possible—as a third direction—to take knowledge as the independent variable rather than the dependent, and to inquire into its social consequences rather than its social causes. This is one of the tasks to which Judith Willer's book makes a major contribution. She explores with sense and sophistication the operation of knowledge, or what she calls knowledge systems, in the ongoing processes of society. She agrees with Francis Bacon's equation of knowledge with power, and shows how this power becomes a significant factor in the social structure. Knowledge, incidentally, as she well knows, does not need to be "true" in order to exert an effect. Thus, the false proposition that the birth of twins is *ipso facto* evidence of adultery can result in the corporal punishment of the mother in a primitive society. The false notion that one race of mankind is innately inferior to another can have devastating consequences in societies we like to think of as other than primitive. The author fully appreciates the force of W.I. Thomas's observation that when men define situations as real they are real in their consequences.

Judith Willer is especially able to apply this principle to the materials she chooses to treat. At the same time that she makes incisive distinctions between magic, religion, and science, she recognizes that all three are forms of knowledge and that all of them have social consequences. Finally, she is worried that science itself, including technology, may assume in the twentieth century some of the attributes of magic in an earlier time, and possibly exercise a pernicious effect upon human welfare in a contemporary society.

This book, in short, extends the mind. It is at once scholarly and fascinating—two adjectives that infrequently belong together. The author is clearly in command of her materials, her insights are ingenious and penetrating, and she has given us a superior contribution to sociological discourse.

Robert Bierstedt
New York University

CHAPTER ONE

THE THEORETICAL UNDERSTANDING OF SOCIAL KNOWLEDGE

Many scholars equate magic with superstition, religion with speculation about the unknown, and science with careful empirical observation. As such, these kinds of knowledge are often regarded as universal elements of social structures. Knowledge in any society is thought to have components of superstition, speculation, and careful observation which correspond respectively to psychological states of ignorance, insecurity, and intelligence. According to this point of view, society has different types of knowledge which vary with its different types of individuals and the diverse situations in which they find themselves.

Nevertheless there are distinctions between magic, religion, and science which cannot be accounted for merely by reference to the particular situations in which they are found. Magical knowledge is not found simply in situations in which individuals are ignorant of the *true* explanation. Whole societies may rely on magical knowledge for all explanations and direction of actions. Who is to say that the explanations provided by individuals in other cultures are more true or satisfactory? Our society might regard the magical knowledge of the Hopi Indians as examples of ignorance—we know (or at least think we know) that dancing does not produce rain. But the Hopi know that if they dance long enough it will eventually rain. Constant empirical association of dancing followed by rain may verify their position for them. They may trust the evidence of their eyes more than they trust the claims of our meteorologists. Their belief in the efficacy of the rain dance is based on empirical observation. But this corresponds exactly to the notion that science is based on careful empirical observation. Obviously this distinction between magic and science is not adequate in some situations. Magical actions usually cannot be explained by simply classifying them as founded in ignorance.

As long as magical, religious, and scientific knowledge are distinguished only through reference to particular situations, their meaning will remain ambiguous. Theoretically useful definitions will not appear by themselves. It is clear to us that the Hopi explanation is based on magical knowledge while the meteorologist bases his explanation on scientific knowledge, but it is equally clear that these terms have gained their meaning from our perception of the empirical situation. Our conceptions depend too strongly on the particular empirical situation which we are presently describing. It is a mistake to assume that the best definitions of types of knowledge will emerge automatically from an increasingly broader acquaintance with the "facts."

The collection of masses of empirical data variously related to a phenomenon is sometimes simplified by classification. Classification adds nothing to the data but simplifies our perception of it. But classification must be accurate. We cannot classify religions as either "evaluative" or "cognitive," for example, if some are both evaluative and cognitive and some are neither. To say that some are evaluative, some are cognitive, some are both, and some are neither, is no doubt an inclusive categorization; but the distinctions do not appear to be very useful.

The problems faced by distinctions which are tied to empirical situations are complicated when they are described as universal social phenomena. Malinowski, for example, designated magic, religion, and science as universal social phenomena.[1] This assertion is seldom questioned. Students of religion, in particular, usually accept it without question.[2] Perhaps, now that institutionalized religion in the United States appears to be on the wane, it is time to question it, not simply on empirical grounds (its "truth") but on the basis of its very meaning.

The claim that magic, religion, and science are universal social phenomena may mean:

(A) that "society" is defined by the presence of magic, religion, and

---

[1] See Bronislaw Malinowski, *Magic, Science and Religion and Other Essays* (Garden City: Doubleday & Company, 1955), p. 17.

[2] Elizabeth Nottingham, for example, writes: "The universality of religious behavior among human beings may for practical purposes be assumed." *Religion and Society* (New York: Random House, 1963), p. 1. See also Joachim Wach, *Sociology of Religion* (Chicago: The University of Chicago Press, 1944), p. 376 and the discussion by Talcott Parsons of social structures in *The Social System* (Glencoe: The Free Press, 1951), pp. 151–67. Parsons, of course, presents his work in the form of empirical generalizations which are consistently ambiguous; and in this case it is difficult to tell whether he actually means religion is a universal integrating force or whether, like the statements of the Greek oracles, his discussion is left open for either interpretation according to the reader's preference.

science; however, no entity may be identified as a society if we do not have rigorous definitions of those terms.

On the other hand, the assertion may mean:

(B) that wherever societies are found we always find magic, religion, and science present.

Regardless of whether the statement that all societies have these phenomena is definitional of societies or an empirical generalization about them, it can have no empirical application without conceptual differentiation between magic, religion, and science, and perhaps other phenomena which might be confused with these concepts. The universality of religion, magic, or science is therefore an empty assertion. Unless the concept of religion is adequately defined, its use can be expected to lead to accumulated errors. To draw conclusions from an assumption of universality with no empirical validity is a risky procedure, the conclusions having no more validity than the assumption itself. As long as these terms remain undefined, as long as we have no specific criteria by which we can distinguish them and definitely point them out as specific phenomena, we cannot empirically validate any statement linking them with other social phenomena.

If magic, religion, and science represent distinct types of social knowledge, their definition must be isomorphic to observable phenomena; but if it is to explain those phenomena, it must consist of more than their empirical characteristics. A good theoretical definition of types of knowledge in society will not only possess isomorphism with empirical events, but the concepts will be unambiguously related to other concepts in order to provide an explanation for those events. Thus theoretical definitions of magic, religion, and science should possess meaning beyond that provided by empirical generalization or association, which will form the basis of explanation.

Magic, religion, and science, if considered theoretically as systems of knowledge, will correspond to definite phenomenological conditions. In this way the universality of the theoretical definitions of these types of systems of knowledge is gained by means of a logical strategy, a deliberate construction, which implies a particular empirical approach. Universality in theory does not emerge from data collection but is derived from the theoretical approach itself. Because theories are stated in terms not limited to particular cultures, because they do not arise from empirical generalization which is tied to the cultures upon which it is based, they transcend particular cultures. Their universality is therefore a result of their nature as mental constructs. Distinguishing between types of knowledge theoretically, then, does not consist of empirical categorization (which is both culture bound and ambiguous). Instead, types of knowledge are clearly separated by means of an unambiguous theoretical system. In Einstein's words:

> Science is the attempt to make the chaotic diversity of our sense-experience correspond to a logically uniform system of thought. In this system single experi-

ences must be correlated with the theoretic structure in such a way that the resulting coordination is unique and convincing.

The sense-experiences are the given subject matter. But the theory that shall interpret them is man-made. It is the result of an extremely laborious process of adaptation: hypothetical, never completely final, always subject to question and doubt.[3]

In presenting a theory of types of social knowledge, it would be convenient if that theory would correspond to our common sense distinctions between magic, religion, and science. It is probable that, despite the ambiguity involved in these rather loose common sense definitions, there is inherent in them some point of view which may be isolated to form the basis of a theoretical distinction. The theoretical definition of systems of knowledge will begin with the question: from what point of view (or system of knowledge) are events observed? If everyone wore green spectacles, all observations might lead to a conception of a green world. In a similar way, perception from the viewpoint of a system of knowledge would affect observation and consequent action.

Max Gluckman has spoken of magical beliefs with reference to a "system": "the African cannot see that the system is untrue and moreover he has to reason with the system as we do with our scientific beliefs. Wherever the system might conflict with reality its beliefs are vague, and deal with transcendent non-observable facts."[4] Here he has noted the similarity of magic and science as systems but has not perceived that viewing behavior and beliefs as consequences of a system of knowledge eliminates the question of "truth" or "falsity." A belief is either consistent or inconsistent with a system of knowledge, and what is regarded as "true" in terms of one system may be "false" for another.

Magical, mystical, religious, and scientific systems of knowledge will be defined in a later section as logically exclusive, but they are not said to be logically exhaustive. Empirical manifestations of systems of knowledge are not expected to conform to the "pure" theoretical definitions presented, but the characteristics of each type should be clearly distinguishable in every case. A system of knowledge determines how an individual relates himself to and describes himself within his empirical surroundings. Because it describes man's relation to the world, it determines his perception. A system of knowledge must be understood in terms of the social structure in which it is found and thus should be compatible with it. Man's actions in the world will be determined by his conception of his place in this social structure. The primary concern here is with systems of knowledge, but this does not

---

[3] Albert Einstein, *Out of My Later Years* (New York: Philosophical Library, 1950), p. 98.

[4] Max Gluckman, "The Logic of African Science and Witchcraft: An Appreciation of Evans-Pritchard's *Witchcraft Oracles and Magic Among the Azande* of the Sudan," *Rhodes-Livingstone Institute Journal*, June 1944, p. 67.

mean that the ideas of those systems will be thought of as more powerful causes of behavior than conditions of existence. Exact explanation of human behavior requires consideration of both.

Ideas and social conditions are not completely independent of each other, but neither is there a simplistic relationship between them. Usually types of knowledge and types of social structures will demonstrate an isomorphism, a similarity of structure.

This work is theoretical; the theory and the facts for it are clearly distinguished. Theory provides generality without the ambiguity of empirical generalization because it is rationally constructed to be exact. Theory thus makes exact differentiation between phenomena possible. But, even more importantly, theory provides an objectivity not possible when analysis is made solely on the basis of our perceptions. Systems of knowledge are highly concerned with values about which the researcher may have opinions, and he is faced with the problem of remaining value-neutral under these conditions. Without formal concepts, he must view other cultures in terms common to his own. This necessarily introduces bias, in spite of the best of intentions. The use of formal theory which we check for isomorphism with the empirical world and do not believe in as a truth, makes objectivity at least possible. The meaning of theoretical concepts is fixed in advance of consideration of a culture, and the elements of the culture are then considered for isomorphism with the theoretical concepts. If this isomorphism is not found, the theory must be revised or rejected and checked again for isomorphism. The gaining of objectivity in the study of knowledge is in itself sufficient reason for the choice of a theoretical method.

CHAPTER TWO

MALINOWSKI: SCIENCE AMONG THE SAVAGES

Magic, religion, and science, according to Malinowski, are universal social phenomena:

> There are no peoples however primitive without religion and magic. Nor are there, it must be added at once, any savage races lacking either in the scientific attitude or in science, though this lack has been frequently attributed to them.[1]

This was a revolutionary statement. Before Malinowski expressed this opinion, it was assumed by cultural historians that science was characteristic only of complex societies and that the incidence of magic was extremely limited in modern Western civilizations. Nevertheless, this statement carries little conviction without the extensive elaboration of historical cases necessary to establish the claim of universality. His discussion also suffers in that he defined science so loosely that even a cookbook could be described as scientific since it consists of "a body of rules and conceptions, based on experience and derived from it by logical inference."[2] He called this a "minimum" definition, and he appears to have been right in that opinion; however, it must be used here in the search for support of his notion of science as rules and conceptions derived from experience.

In a typical example he claimed that "The native shipwright knows

[1] Bronislaw Malinowski, *Magic, Science and Religion and Other Essays* (Garden City: Doubleday & Company, 1955), p.17.

[2] *Ibid.*, p. 34.

not only practically of bouyancy, leverage, equilibrium, he has to obey these laws."[3] If he meant that native shipwrights were acquainted with the relevant scientific laws, the evidence is inaccurate and does not support his notion of "savage science." These particular scientific laws were developed only once. The laws of levers and bouyancy were both formulated by Archimedes. (It is not clear what the "law" of equilibrium is.) In fact, when it is realized that Archimedes had the Greek, Egyptian, and Mesopotamian written cultural traditions to draw upon in formulating these laws, Malinowski's assertion is simply untenable. His interpretation appears to arbitrarily project the ideas of his own culture into another, a procedure which anthropologists frequently caution against.

If Malinowski did not really mean that the natives were acquainted with scientific laws, what other interpretation would make sense in this context? Perhaps by "laws" he meant merely the assumption of the absolute uniformity of nature and the consequent necessity of conforming to it or "obeying" it. Perhaps (since he limited science to the empirical domain) he meant no more than that; when primitive shipwrights build ships to get from place to place over the water, they have to build them so that they will not immediately sink, break apart, or turn turtle. If so, these facts are not surprising. If disasters occurred regularly, the specialization of shipwright undoubtedly would not have developed among the Trobriands or would have been shortly done away with (and a good many shipwrights with it). But if this is all the statement means, it is misleading. The ability of "savages" to build ships that float has no more to do with the understanding of scientific laws than does the effectiveness of a cook depend upon the understanding of modern chemistry.

It should be noted that the idea of the native having to "obey" scientific laws is meaningless unless one is convinced that nature is uniform and that scientific laws are "discovered" from its study and must be conformed to. If one admits that science is changeable and theoretical, one does not expect to obey its laws.

If the primitive does not have and cannot use systematic science, perhaps he can be viewed as a "natural" scientist. He undoubtedly is "patient and painstaking in his observations, capable of generalization and of connecting long chains of events in the life of animals and in the marine world or in the jungle."[4] But, to the extent that natural science is limited to observation, generalization, and simple empirical connection, it is prescientific because it lacks both theories and laws. Those acts which Malinowski classified as "scientific" can not be separated in fact from magic as he claimed they could. This claim is not supported by ethnographic evidence. What Westerners appre-

[3] *Ibid.*, p. 34.
[4] *Ibid.*, p. 35.

hend as magic is not separated from other types of behavior by the primitive himself. Magic is seen to have practical ends inseparable from what we might call technological knowledge and what Malinowski calls science. Magical acts are often separated by the observer from other acts because he knows they will not produce the desired end, but this is not to say that the primitive shares this knowledge. Of course, conventional Western impressions, when they do not correspond to the notions of the primitives themselves, hinder rather than help in the explanation of primitive behavior.

Malinowski consistently maintained that savages have both empirical and rational knowledge, but he indicated that science in primitive societies is not a "driving power, criticizing, renewing, constructing."[5] In other words, it has no rational component. But, if it is limited to empiricism, it is not science if science is admitted to have a rational, theoretical, component. Evidence that primitives have science of this sort is plainly lacking. They are not observed to have the effects of science: high population density, complex technical developments with associated methods of symbolic representation, and complex division of labor. If primitive society exhibited these characteristics, it would not be considered primitive.

Science is not even *developed* in semi-isolated, technologically simple, preliterate societies. This does not mean, however, that "savages" carry out their actions in ignorance—their behavior is based upon knowledge quite comparable to that of the average modern man in his average action. Present day civilized man, although he may freely use the products of science and its technology, rarely disciplines his thinking with scientific laws. Malinowski confused science with the ability to intelligently cope with the environment: "Science . . . is based on the normal universal experience of everyday life, experience won in man's struggle with nature for his subsistence and safety, founded on observation, fixed by reason."[6] What he did not appear to realize is that an individual may cope effectively without science. Moreover, if one adhered closely to his conception of science as based on the normal experience of everyday life, then Galileo should not have needed the telescope nor Lawrence the cloud chamber, and their theoretical developments would not have taken place at all since they were not based on man's concern with his struggle for subsistence.

Here again, Malinowski projected his Western point of view on the thinking of a quite different society. His empirical interpretation of science in Western society became the basis for attributing science to the savages.

In spite of his circumscribed notion of magic (narrowed because of his ambiguous notion of science), Malinowski's description of magical practices is of great interest. He pointed out, for example, that magic is "an entirely

[5] *Ibid.*, p. 35.
[6] *Ibid.*, p. 87.

sober, prosaic, even clumsy art, enacted for purely practical reasons, governed by crude and shallow beliefs, carried out in simple and monotonous technique."[7] This observation is valuable for pointing out the mistake of the occult and esoteric notion of magic so prevalent in Western society. This mistaken notion seems to have had its source in the Christian condemnation of native European magic and not in the prevailing character of magic itself. Indeed, Malinowski carried his analysis further to distinguish magic from religion by the "purely practical," "means to an end" nature of the former.[8] As far as it goes, this distinction appears to be accurate.

> Follow one rite, study one spell, grasp the principles of magical belief, art and sociology in one case, and you will know not only all the acts of the tribe, but, adding a variant here and there, you will be able to settle as a magical practitioner in any part of the world.[9]

The most widespread magical act of all, according to Malinowski, is the pointing of the magical dart, the purpose being to inflict harm by action at a distance. The dart is pointed at the victim and is accompanied by a show of intense feeling. This may be understood as an empirical analogy to a projectile, as "imitative" magic with the accompanying projecting of feeling. But under some circumstances, it is clear that the act might be thought of as efficacious.

For Malinowski, magic is false knowledge: "Plausible though the fallacious claims of magic might be to primitive man, how is it that they have remained so long unexposed?"[10] The question for Malinowski was not what criterion of belief is utilized in magic which is different from that used in science or religion, but how is it that these savages can remain so long in error? The answer he gave to this question was partly physiological and partly social-psychological—the essence of magic is emotion.[11] Therefore, he claimed, magical acts can be explained in terms of: "reactions to overwhelming emotion or obsessive desire [which] are natural responses of man to such a situation, based on a universal psycho-physiological mechanism."[12] In addition, "a positive case always overshadows the negative one"[13] and the savage therefore does not see his error. Finally, magic is wielded only by special men, "men of great intelligence, energy, and power of enterprise. . . . It is an empirical fact that in all savage societies magic and outstanding

[7] *Ibid.*, p. 70.
[8] See *ibid.*, p. 70.
[9] *Ibid.*, p. 70.
[10] *Ibid.*, p. 82.
[11] See *ibid.*, p. 71.
[12] *Ibid.*, p. 80.
[13] *Ibid.*, p. 82.

personality go hand in hand."[14] ". . . No wonder that it is considered a source of success."[15]

Here, a magical act is explained by claiming that it is an expression of emotion; and emotion is explained as a "universal psycho-physiological mechanism." In other words, Malinowski assumed the general in order to explain the particular. All evidence for the general is, of course, lacking. In fact, it seems singularly peculiar that magic could have declined in modern civilization if it indeed rests on a universal something-or-other.

Still, the very maintenance of "false" knowledge requires explanation. Malinowski's explanations of the retention of magical knowledge can be summarized as: (1) the universal tendency to accentuate the positive, and (2) the power of cultural superheroes. That empirical evidence does or could establish the hypothesis that successful experiences are remembered and unsuccessful ones forgotten is doubtful; even that would not explain the maintenance of specifically magical knowledge but would only explain the maintenance of any kind of presently existing knowledge. The tendency to accentuate the positive thus can *explain no particular* type of thinking. If it exists, it should be relevant to every successful thought ever conceived by man. On the other hand, if magic is false, it might instead be a basis for its rejection. The role of the cultural superhero is even more questionable. Malinowski appears to have said no more than that those who are outstandingly successful by the values of a culture are thought to be adroit at using the means of power conceived by the culture. This does not explain why "false" knowledge is maintained. It says only that some individuals are more successful than others in using it. This argues more for a revolution in thought than maintenance, particularly when the less successful outnumber the successful. In fact, it explains nothing at all.

The fault lies, of course, in Malinowski's notion of magic as false knowledge. Magic is not thought of as false by those who use it (although some may be skeptical of its use). It would appear that the truth or falsity of magical knowledge must be judged by the criteria of magical knowledge, not by the criteria of some other type of knowledge. If Malinowski's criticism of magical knowledge had been based on some theory of truth encompassing all criteria of knowledge in all societies, its basis would have at least been reasonable, but to claim the criteria of knowledge to be wrong in another culture because they do not conform to those of our own is a dubious logical procedure. That magical knowledge is false by the criteria of religious or scientific knowledge is not immediately relevant to the acts of its "savage" practitioner any more than a criticism of science as false in his (the savage's)

---

[14] *Ibid.*, p. 83.
[15] *Ibid.*, p. 83.

terms would be to the scientist. The only implication this disagreement of criteria of truth has is in the possibility of conflict when the different criteria come into contact.

Malinowski defined religion as "a body of self-contained acts being themselves the fulfillment of their purpose."[16] The nature of religion, then, is not parallel to magic and science which are described as means to ends. Perhaps the statement could be translated to say that in religion means are identical to ends, motives being no more than actions in accordance with the value system. But to say that the search for salvation is motivated only by religious values does not appear different in form from the statement that the search for power is motivated only by magical values. Just as the notion of religious salvation depends on the religion, the notion of magical power depends on the magic. If one way of thinking and doing is thus self-contained, so is the other.

Religion gives the superficial impression of being more self-contained than magic. It is viewed as having its own domain, the sacred, which poses motives counter to those common in the domain of the profane. But the motives of magic appear similar to those of the profane, and thus to the Western mind it appears as if religion has drawn a line around a small part of thinking, separating it off from the profane which includes all other thinking (and thus magic).

Malinowski's conceptions of magic, science, and religion are unclear and inadequate to indicate what phenomena he wishes to delineate by which term. His own examples do not appear to support his conceptions. His "theory" often declines to universal postulates of psychological or physiological reductionism. His "theory" seems much closer to explanation through hasty generalization from the empirical than to any scientific explanation. It was through his identification of magic with science, his lack of theoretical separation of the terms, that he was able to find science among the savages.

Malinowski's conceptions of magic, science, and religion drew heavily from the work of Frazer. Many of the problems with Malinowski's conceptions were inherited from Frazer by adoption of his viewpoint. From Frazer's point of view, magic's "fundamental conception is identical with that of modern science; underlying the whole system is a faith, implicit but real and firm, in the order and uniformity of nature."[17] But magic is false science:

> The fatal flaw of magic lies not in its general assumption of a sequence of events determined by law, but in its total misconception of the nature of the particular laws which govern that sequence. . . . The principles of association are excellent in themselves, and indeed absolutely essential to the working of the

[16] *Ibid.*, p. 88.
[17] Sir James G. Frazer, *The Golden Bough: A Study in Magic and Religion*, abridged edition (New York: The Macmillan Company, 1958), p. 56.

human mind. Legitimately applied they yield science; illegitimately applied they yield magic, the bastard sister of science. It is therefore a truism, almost a tautology, to say that all magic is necessarily false and barren; for were it ever to become true and fruitful, it would not longer be magic but science.[18]

In fact, Frazer offered explanations for the maintenance of this false knowledge which, although less fantastic than Malinowski's, were no more satisfactory. But Frazer did not make the error of assuming that science is therefore present in primitive cultures side by side with magic. Neither did Frazer believe that religion is a universal cultural trait. Instead he believed that magic predated religion:

> Yet though magic is thus found to fuse and amalgamate with religion in many ages and in many lands, there are some grounds for thinking that this fusion is not primitive, and that there was a time when man trusted to magic alone for the satisfaction of such wants as transcend his immediate animal cravings. In the first place a consideration of the fundamental notions of magic and religion may incline us to surmise that magic is older than religion in the history of humanity.[19]

If religion developed after magic, then there were some peoples without religion, and Malinowski was wrong. Frazer's claim is more satisfactory, if for no other reason than the fact that his definition of religion is more satisfactory. Religion is "a propitiation or conciliation of powers superior to man which are believed to direct and control the course of nature and of human life. Thus defined, religion consists of two elements, a theoretical and a practical."[20] Here the distinction between religion and magic has two bases. First, religion, unlike magic, has a theoretic component commonly called a theology.[21] Magic has no theoretic component whatsoever but is instead thoroughly practical. Secondly, magic and religion differ in the distribution of power. While in magic man may possess powers, in religion powers are reserved for superior beings. According to Frazer, religion and magic are in conflict because the magician usurps powers for himself which the religious man believes are "prerogatives that belong to God alone."[22]

If Malinowski had borrowed Frazer's conception of religion rather than his distinction between magic and science, his analysis might have fit his facts better. Most of the contrasts Frazer drew between magic and religion appear to be accurate and to demonstrate a clear conceptualization of the two as different phenomena. The main problem with Frazer's ideas is in the meaning he attributed to "science." Because his definition of science does not

---

[18] *Ibid.*, p. 57.
[19] *Ibid.*, p. 62.
[20] *Ibid.*, pp. 57–58.
[21] See *ibid.*, p. 58.
[22] *Ibid.*, p. 60.

fit with the notion that theory is included in science in addition to empirical observation, he found it necessary to define magic as "false" in order to separate the two.

Science appeared to Frazer to have the same logical basis as magic. It was logically unlike religion because religion has a theoretic component. Thus, according to Frazer, science is a completely empirical undertaking. Along with other British Empiricists (such as Locke, Hume, Mill, and Pearson) Frazer limited scientific knowledge to what can be observed by use of the senses. But the assumptions that go along with the notion of science without theory, such as the assumption of the uniformity of nature, are not assumptions of modern science at all.

If it is realized that science and magic may be separated because of the presence of theory in the former, it is no longer necessary to call magical knowledge "false" in order to differentiate it from scientific knowledge. Magic may instead be considered to be knowledge of a different kind.

CHAPTER THREE

THE STRUCTURE
OF KNOWLEDGE
SYSTEMS

Systems of knowledge are concerned with the nature of the world. A system of knowledge dictates thinking about the world and action in relation to it. Simple societies by definition contain only one system of knowledge; complex societies contain more than one. Individuals in the same society will necessarily share the same system of thought only if the society is simple, while in complex societies individuals may share a language but not a common knowledge system. On the other hand, knowledge systems can be translated from one language to another and transported from society to society.

Systems of knowledge dictate thinking and action concerned with the nature of the world and are limited to this subject only. Habitual actions, customary actions, and other ordinary day-to-day activities do not usually call up questions about the nature of the world or require explanations of connections in the world and are not subjects of concern for systems of knowledge. But when such actions are thought to be concerned with the nature of the world they are relevant to the dictates of the system of knowledge.

Because systems of knowledge are concerned with the world and are held by men who must use them for certain explanations and substantiations for their actions, they must explain the connection of one circumstance to another. The ability to connect circumstance A to circumstance B is defined as *power*. It explains the nature of the actions which may be taken by individuals to get from A to a desired B. Concern with relations in the world is simultaneously a concern with power since power is the specification of the dynamics of the relationship of A and B.

A system of knowledge is nothing more than a set of ideas about the nature of the world and the relationships in it. Systems of knowledge are collections of explanations of the relatedness of A and B (or C and D, etc.) which have been needed either to explain or predict B or to determine what to do to get from circumstance A to B. Individual explanations of events will differ according to the different systems of knowledge. For example, the appearance of the moon might be explained as the result of its own power to move or the power of another individual to move it in a magical system of knowledge, as the result of the action of an all-powerful God in a religious system, or as a result of the combination of observable qualities with a rational system of explanation involving concepts such as "mass" and "force" in a scientific system. Death, likewise, might be explained as the result of an individual magical act, the Will of God, or certain conditions of the body as they are related to death by medical science.

The latter example can be used to illustrate how explanations and behavior are related. Some magical systems relate death to the action of witches. If all death is due to the power of a witch, then the individual who wants the assurance of long life should be sure never to offend a witch or, alternatively, should accumulate enough power to be safe. In a religious system where death is a result of the will of an omnipotent god, the individual cannot influence his time of death. But religious systems with omnipotent gods may also contain a belief in life after death. Here the motivation evidenced in a magical system as a desire for long life becomes instead a concern with salvation for eternal life. From the point of view of medical science, the condition of an individual body may be analyzed in terms of medical concepts relating to the functioning of a healthy body, and the individual might influence the length of his life by acting in accordance with those concepts. He might, for example, avoid smoking cigarettes in order to lessen his chances of getting cancer.

If two or more explanations are contradictory, one or the other may, depending upon whether these bits of knowledge are ever connected in the thought of one individual, eventually be rejected. Some types of knowledge systems may be expected to continually undergo rationalization while others may lead to new connections only under the pressure of circumstances; but the retention of contradictory explanations is dependent upon their isolation from one another. Nevertheless, there is no necessity for two separate explanations in a system to be logically related. The relatedness of A and B may imply nothing about C and D, but *if it does*, the implication will be consistent from the point of view of the system of knowledge in which it is found. If, for example, A is acted upon in a certain manner leading to B and through more action to C, the system will not include the thought that A cannot be connected with C.

A system of knowledge therefore consists of no more than thoughts about the relatedness of mental and observational notions. Actions which do not require reflection about relatedness do not call upon the individual to refer to a system of knowledge. Systems of knowledge may at times be implicit when the individual undertakes an action requiring some thought about the connection of A and B but does not reflect upon the connection since the connection has been made through previous reflection (either by that individual or someone else). Therefore an individual may carry out a certain action to obtain condition B without immediate conscious awareness of the nature of its connection with A. On the other hand, an action may be taken with the connections provided by the system of knowledge consciously used. In this case the knowledge system is explicit.

Perception of order in empirical situations is based on the type of system of knowledge used, and it follows that experiences will not contradict it. Sensations are categorized by the system of knowledge and thus are not tests of it, although they may lead to its modification. The continuation of a rain dance for an extended period might eventually lead to doubts as to the correctness of the procedure as it was carried out or to the notion that some counteraction is being taken against the production of rain, but it is not likely to lead to the rejection of the notion that rain dances produce rain. Doubt as to the accuracy of this explanation is likely to occur only from the point of view of an individual with an alternative explanation which is part of a different knowledge system. Experience thus will not cause the adherents to a system of knowledge to reject the system, but they may modify parts of it in order to make the system as a whole more useful. The type of system of knowledge is determined by the types of thought which may make it up.

TYPES OF THOUGHT CONNECTION

Different knowledge systems are connected to specific types of thought: empirical, rational, or abstractive. Magical knowledge may thus be differentiated from religious, mystical, or scientific knowledge because the type of thought which is characteristic of it is distinct from the types of thought which prevail in societies characterized by the other systems of knowledge. Combinations of the three basic types of thought connection determine all knowledge. Systems of knowledge will derive from these types of connection and their combinations. The three basic types of connection are represented in Table 1. They are differentiated by the levels at which connections in thinking are made. A connection which is initiated and concluded only at the observational level is termed *empirical*. It is indicated by the search for

TABLE 1. Basic Types of Thought Connection.

Connective Level	Types of Thought Connection		
Theoretic		Rational a-----→b	Abstractive $\begin{array}{c} \text{A}\text{-}\text{-}\text{-}\text{-}\text{→b} \\ \text{or} \\ \text{B}\text{-}\text{-}\text{-}\text{a} \end{array}$
Observational	Empirical A-----→B		

causes and effects through observation only. Empirical thinking always connects observable to observable. It is manifested in the works of some philosophers and social observers by their assertions that they want to describe "what is really there." The connection of observable circumstance A to observable circumstance B follows various rules. For example, if B follows A in time, one may say A *causes* B. Or the empirical *generalization* may be made that all A is followed by B and the deductive connection made that this A will be followed by a B. Of course, if the predicted event does not take place, the empirical thinker will conclude that either the generalization was wrong (which is equivalent to saying it does not work) or that this case has not been a typical one or has been subject to more influences than that of A.

Alternatively, empirical connections may be expressed by statistical relations such as the correlation of As with Bs. Empirical connections are not merely made by association of A and B over time but by other observable associations as well.

Perhaps the best known example of empirical thought is to be found in the work of David Hume. Hume divided "perceptions of the mind" into two classes: the less forcible—thoughts and ideas; and the more forcible—impressions. Impressions include what we hear, see, feel, and will. Thoughts are less forcible because no object can be represented with as great vigor in an idea as it can when directly perceived. It was Hume's contention that, although thought seems to possess unbounded liberty, "it is really confined within very narrow limits . . . (to) . . . compounding, transposing, augmenting, or diminishing the materials afforded us by the senses and experience."[1] To think of a golden mountain means no more than to compound the ideas of gold and mountain whose meaning we are acquainted with by previous experience. Hume offered two arguments intended to prove this assertion. In the first he maintained that when thoughts or ideas are analyzed, regardless of their complexity, "they resolve themselves into such simple ideas as were copied from a precedent feeling or sentiment."[2] Even the idea of God

[1] David Hume, *An Enquiry Concerning Human Understanding* (Chicago: Gateway Editions, Inc., 1956), p. 16.
[2] *Ibid.*, p. 17.

arises as a consequence of "operations of our mind"[3] which can be traced back to experience. Hume argued that "If it happen, from a defect of the organ, that a man is not susceptible of any species of sensation, we always find that he is as little susceptible of the correspondent ideas."[4] But, he contended, if that defect were repaired and that sense restored, the man would be rendered capable of understanding the ideas corresponding to that sense.

An important part of Hume's empirical thinking is his discussion of necessary connection. He appears to have taken the position that mathematics has the advantage over the study of morals in that the terms of the former are unambiguous, and this lack of ambiguity he attributed to the immediacy of sense data: "If any term be defined in geometry, the mind readily, in itself, substitutes, on all occasions, the definition for the term defined: or even when no definition is employed, the object itself may be presented to the senses, and by that means be steadily and clearly apprehended."[5] The position that the terms of mathematics are immediately definable in terms of sense perceptions is consistent with his general position, but it differs from the modern conception that the terms of mathematics or any formal theory cannot be reduced to sense operations. If, as Plato pointed out, there is no perfectly straight line in nature, Hume's statement that the terms of geometry are clear because we can refer them to sense data, appears wrong. The definition of a straight line cannot be derived from any empirical object because lines as straight as those implied by our mental conception have not been (or cannot be) observed.

"There are," according to Hume, "no ideas, which occur in metaphysics more obscure and uncertain, than those of *power, force, energy* or *necessary connection.*"[6] The first man to see motion given by impulse of one billiard ball on another could only say that the two were conjoined. He could not claim that they were necessarily connected. "But when one particular species of event has always, in all instances been conjoined with another . . . We then call one object, *cause;* the other, *effect.* . . . It appears, then, that this idea of a necessary connection among events arises from a number of similar instances which occur of the constant conjunction of these events."[7] In other words, "cause" and "effect" are labels for the association of terms in an empirical generalization, the connection of which has no necessity beyond habit.

Such an analysis cuts through a great mass of mental garbage by offering a practical and sensible solution to a perplexing problem; but, interestingly, and possibly in spite of itself, modern science has not followed Hume's

[3] *Ibid.*, p. 17.
[4] *Ibid.*, p. 18.
[5] *Ibid.*, p. 63.
[6] *Ibid.*, p. 64.
[7] *Ibid.*, p. 80.

meaning. The idea of necessity which is a feature of the conception of cause is not empirical necessity, but the logical necessity of theoretical connection. Hume carried the idea of necessary connection to its logical conclusion from the point of view of empirical thinking; but the typical empirical thinker may accept this idea as true because of the fact that it is sufficient in most cases to rely on appearances alone, and the connection *appears* necessary. At the same time, Western thought contains a notion of necessary connection which is not dependent on empirical thinking.

Hume, indeed, was a pure and consistent empiricist and, as such, his ideas acquired a considerable following and had a remarkable impact on Western thought. It is, moreover, important to realize that Hume's empiricism was quite self-conscious. It was self-consciously developed in Western culture where other types of thought were known and deliberately rejected for it. Most empirical thinking, however, does not result from a conscious rejection of other types of thinking. It is possible that no other types will be known to some people who use only empirical thought. Thinking concerned with technology and its application, in primitive cultures and even through the Renaissance in Western thought, has typically been empirical. Most economic thought and economic behavior has also been empirical. The majority of human thought throughout history may, in fact, be of this simplest type.

The sorts of explanations we give for everyday occurrences are of this type. If a child were to ask why the sugar disappeared when it was put in the tea, the answer he would probably be given is that sugar dissolves in water, an empirical explanation. Its empirical character is demonstrated in the terms (sugar, dissolves, and water), all of which are observables, and in the basis of its connection, observation. Because lightening and thunder are observed together time after time, and because the former precedes the latter, one concludes that lightening causes thunder, an empirical conclusion which may, in turn, be used to explain future individual occurrences of thunder.

Explanations given for everyday events usually are empirical. They are distinguished by the exclusive use of observational terms and by the rationale for the connection of these terms which is also observational.

Rationality, on the other hand, is a type of thought which makes connections only at the theoretic level. It is initiated at the theoretic level and concluded there. It works therefore in terms of mentally constructed systems of concepts. Mathematical and metaphysical systems are both rationalistic. There is no need to refer to observables to think with either. One may ask a rationalistic question about the sum of 48 and 73 and arrive at the conclusion that it is 121 without ever having made references to observables. The numbers and mental operation of summing are both parts of the rational mathematical system.

Beginning with Plato (who was the first to consciously use concepts), Western knowledge has contained a component, according to Northrop, which "cannot be gained or justified directly by mere factual observation or direct introspection."[8] This knowledge is not of observables but of the unseen. Northrop called this element (which is here referred to as rational thought) the "theoretic" component. He claimed that the basic conceptions of Christian theology are concepts of the theoretic component. The meaning of ideas such as "God," "grace," and "revelation," is not given empirically because, like all theoretic ideas, their meaning is not directly dependent on empirical considerations. This conception of Western religion extends beyond Christianity to include Judaism and Islam, although Northrop does not discuss the latter two at any length. From this point of view Western theology has remained dynamic because it is subject to rational extension. On the other hand, it may help to explain its absolute character in its separation from the empirical.

Rational thought consists of concepts and their mental connection. Any thought connection which relates concept to concept is by definition rational. Conversely, all terms related by rational connection are concepts. The statement that two straight lines parallel to a third straight line are parallel to each other, is a rational statement because of the character of its terms and their connection. A "straight line" is a concept, not an observational category. The "parallel" relation of two straight lines is also a connection made at the theoretic level and not observable. There are no observations which correspond exactly to these terms in meaning. No object in nature is perfectly straight. "Straight" cannot therefore be a label for a commonly observed quality but is instead a rational concept which is more or less approximated when interpreted for empirical occurrences. Much the same discussion would fit the connective, "parallel."

As long as thought remains at the theoretic level, it has no empirical meaning whatsoever and cannot be used to explain empirical occurrences. But this is not to say that under these conditions concepts have no meaning. While the primary meaning of empirical terms is in their connection to observable objects or occurrences, the primary meaning of concepts is in their connection to one another. To define an empirical term is to point out (or at least describe) the objects to which it may be applied. To define the term "cow" I might point to the animal to which it is applied or describe its observable characteristics so that it might be recognized. To define a concept, however, is to point out the other concepts to which it can be related and the form of that relationship. The concept, "straight line," alone is

---

[8] F.S.C. Northrop, *The Meeting of East and West* (New York: Macmillan Company, 1953), pp. 294–95.

meaningless. To describe its parallel relatedness to other straight lines is to give a partial rational interpretation of the meaning of the concept.

Concepts are purposefully empty of intrinsic meaning. Their meaning is wholly extrinsic and comes as a consequence of their connection to other concepts. The rational thinker thus has great freedom of connection at the beginning of his work. Once initial rational connections are made, others must be consistent with them if they are related in a system. If not, the original meaning of the concepts is destroyed. From a rational point of view, the connections made between concepts need only to be internally consistent. No other connective rule need be followed. Nevertheless, it is not often that a thinker is interested in concepts for their own sake.

Abstractive thinking connects the theoretic and observational levels. It may begin at the observational level and conclude at the theoretic level or vice versa. Observables are always connected to nonobservables in abstraction, empirical terms to rational concepts. The suffering of a cancer victim (observational level) may thus be explained by the disfavor of God (theoretic level). Good, evil, God, mass, straight line, salvation, etc., are concepts at the theoretic level, and, as such, they are not observables. If such concepts are to have any use (other than their use in rational connection for its own sake) they must be connected to empirical indicators by abstraction. Empirical thought uses only observables, rational thought uses only mental concepts, and abstraction uses only mental concepts and observables together.

As long as rational thought connections are absent, abstraction is of limited utility. But, once thought connections are made at the theoretic level, they may be usefully connected to empirical terms. As in some Western thought, "good" may have a conceptual meaning as a consequence of its relation to other concepts, but it has no relevance to behavior unless it is given observational interpretation. This interpretation consists of the connection by abstraction of the concepts to one or more observational terms which are labels for objects or events. When an observational term is connected to a concept, it may be called an indicator for it. The "goodness" of Christian souls, for example, might be indicated by charitable acts, while the "mass" of an object may be indicated by the pointer on a spring balance.

If a rational system is to have empirical application, its concepts must be connected by abstraction to empirical indicators for them. Given this connection, the workings of the rational system may be used to explain various empirical occurrences.

THE LOGIC OF KNOWLEDGE SYSTEMS

The three types of thought connection may be combined to form four distinct type of knowledge systems whose content is thus partially determined by the particular types of thought connection involved in each. Table 2 illustrates the types of thought connection associated with magical, religious,

TABLE 2. COMBINATIONS OF TYPES OF THOUGHT CONNECTION IN FOUR TYPES OF KNOWLEDGE SYSTEMS.

	Knowledge System:			
Connective Levels:	Magical	Mystical	Religious	Scientific
Theoretic		b	a- - - -→b	a←- - - →b
		↑	↓	↑ ↑ ↓
Observational	A- - - -→B	A - - - -→B	B	A←- - - →B

mystical, and scientific systems of knowledge. Magical systems of knowledge are characterized by empirical thought alone, religion combines abstraction with rationalism, mysticism makes empirical and abstractive connections, and the combination of all three types of connection is characteristic of scientific systems. Societies may be described as magical, religious, mystical, or scientific only in so far as these respective systems of knowledge prevail within them. Clearly the United States in the twentieth century is not characterized only by adherents to scientific knowledge systems if this definition is accepted. Magic, mysticism, and religion determine the thought connection and consequent action of many. The technician who applies the results of a scientific knowledge system often uses only empirical connection himself, assuming the connection to be only on the observable level since these connections alone are useful to him; therefore, his system of knowledge is much closer to magic than science. In fact, since science combines all three types of thought, they may all be found separately within the system without contradiction. Since scientific knowledge integrates all three types of connection, an individual who utilizes only empiricism, only rationalism, or only abstraction cannot be said to have scientific knowledge; but his limited knowledge may be used in the scientific system.

It is not expected that systems of knowledge will apply to all (or even most) situations encountered in society. Any connections which are not related to consideration of the nature of the world are not relevant to systems of knowledge. The individual who utilizes all three types of connection together in his thinking about the nature of the world but only empiricism in his day-to-day activities may be said to be an adherent to a scientific system of knowledge.

1. MAGICAL KNOWLEDGE. Magical knowledge is empirical, but not all empirical thinking is magical. Since empirical thinking is no more than the connection of condition A with condition B at the observational level,

it will form a portion of thinking in any system of knowledge made up of sensing individuals. Empirical thinking is magical only if this type of thinking alone forms the basis for gaining knowledge about connections in the world. It is evident that empirical thinking may exist quite apart from this concern and thus apart from magical notions of any sort. On the other hand, it is logically possible for all thinking in a society to be empirical. Such a society is defined as possessing a magical system of knowledge.

The elements of a magical system are empirical categories. These categories consist of the *identification* of a symbol with a class of objects. Empirical connections are made by certain "rules of thumb," associations made at the observational level. These associations may be of the "imitative" or "contagious" type as described by Frazer or they may be temporal connections which take the form of an "effect" following from a "cause." The acceptance of the notion that everything has a cause follows from the strict adherence to an empirical orientation. To say that the notion is accepted, however, is not to imply that immediate determination of cause is always possible in individual cases.

Knowledge in a magical system consists of knowing the connection between condition A and condition B, the cause of the change from one condition to another. For any individual, knowledge of causal connections is needed to determine action in pursuit of specific ends. The test of this type of knowledge is strongly dependent upon trial and error. Trial and error methods, when separated from questions of relations in the world, are not limited to magical systems of knowledge. This aspect of empirical thinking is nonmagical, secular, and technological. The use of trial and error manipulations for technological purposes will not, under some social conditions, imply the existence of a magical system. Magical systems utilize trial and error methods because there is no choice; all tests of knowledge must rely on empirical evidence, the only type of evidence possible.

In a magical system when one event follows another, when the first event was intended to result in the second, and when this can be conceptualized by a rule of thumb, then the first event will be considered to be causally connected with the second. As events brought about by individuals are observed to be coupled with intent, there will often be an attribution of intent in other events. The attribution of cause in this sense does not necessarily rest upon replication; but one observation of connection, of one event following another, may be sufficient. If the second event does not follow the first in later observations, it may be thought that the intent was no longer present, the causal connection was broken, or the first event lost its efficacy— its power to produce the second (which is essentially an identical notion). Since magical thinking does not extend beyond empirical connection, the notion of "chance" does not occur in magical systems. On the other hand, if an empirical connection is observed time after time, that consistency may provide a basis for future behavior.

Frazer noted that "If we analyze the principles of thought on which magic is based, they will probably be found to resolve themselves into two: first, that like produces like, or that an effect resembles its cause; and, second, that things which have once been in contact with each other continue to act on each other at a distance after the physical contact has been severed."[9] Here he has presented two other types of empirical association beyond that of association in time. These types of association (which Frazer himself regarded as "errors") are made quite correctly if the accepted basis of thought is empirical. Metaphysical speculation about whether this association *really is* as it was observed would not enter into the picture in a magical knowledge system.

Repetition of an action which is *not* followed by repetition of an expected result does not necessarily lead the magical thinker to an idea of a break in causal connection. Other explanations are possible. Since every event has its cause, it follows that each individual is surrounded by a complex web of causal connections, any of which can intervene between an individual's action and his intended result. Others may intend different results. Events in a world of multiple causation are singularly difficult to anticipate. On the other hand, the reproduction of results requires exact repetition of the original event. Subsequent lack of success can thus be attributed to a lack of success in production of the cause.

Magical knowledge is practical. It may be elaborate, but it is never esoteric. It exists only for use. There is no magical knowledge for its own sake.

If magical knowledge transcends particulars, it is only through empirical generalization taking the form "A, then B." The terms "A" and "B" are empirical categories. Connections of this form are very inefficient mediums of information, an inefficiency compounded because both of the terms are empirical categories. Furthermore, the various empirically connected bits of knowledge are not rationalized and are not connected to others. As a consequence, although it may share terms with others, each empirical generalization is independent and isolated from others. Knowledge remains at the level of the immediately observable. These empirically isolated bits and pieces, although they may be consistently arrived at, cannot be collected into an integrated and consciously consistent system of knowledge. Magical knowledge forms a catalogue whose size is limited by the storage capacity of the society.

Moreover, the lack of ability to transcend the level of observables means that a magical system has no internal dynamics. It cannot move ahead

---

[9] Sir James George Frazer, *The Golden Bough: A Study in Magic and Religion* (New York: The Macmillan Company, 1958), abridged edition, p. 12.

intellectually but may be modified only by the external evidence of observation. Changes are therefore not developmental since new bits of knowledge do not build upon old ones but are merely added to them. Change in magical systems is discontinuous and fragmentary.

2. MYSTICAL KNOWLEDGE. Mystical knowledge, like magical knowledge, depends on empirical thought; but in mystical systems an attempt is made to escape from the empirical world, and thus mystical systems have an additional type of thought—abstraction. Whereas the individual in the magical system accepts the system for what it is observed to be and empirical thought as the sole basis of knowledge, the mystic accepts the evidence of empirical observation but finds that it does not satisfy him.

The elements of a mystical system are empirical categories which are either connected in thought to other empirical categories or to a concept at the theoretic level which represents the antiempirical ideal to which the mystic would like to escape. The world is viewed through observation, and the observed phenomena are regarded as real; but the mystic has a conception of a "good," something better than the observed world, and it is this ideal condition that he wishes to reach. In this sense, mystical systems accept the legitimacy of the empirically made connections but do not accept empirical ends as satisfactory. The conception of an ideal end connected with individuals in an empirical world is abstractive.

Empirical thought makes up the subject matter of perception; but, unlike magic, mystical ends are not practical but are reached through abstraction. Observed worldly causal connections are accurate and not denied, but they are not important. Similarly, connections of concept to concept (as in rational thought) are not made. The mystic ideal is an isolated concept in that it is not connected with others in a rational system. Mystical concepts are formed by an idealization, the raising to the theoretic level of some empirical term. The mystic, therefore, does not involve himself in rationalistic arguments with theologians, metaphysicians, or scientists since these are outside the types of thought included in his system of knowledge.

The mystical concept or goal consists of elevating some notion gained from the world to an ideal position, such as supreme knowledge, supreme happiness, or peace. In this sense, although it is nonworldly in its final conception, it is not defined through its relation to other concepts. The goal is at the theoretic level, the end point of an abstractive process.

The final aim of mysticism is an abstraction of the individual's thought from the observational to a theoretic end state. Since this end state is theoretic and unitary and is not connected to other theoretic ideas, the mystic has great difficulty communicating the meaning of the end state to those who have not themselves attained it. The fact that it is not related to other theoretic concepts makes this communication difficult but does not mean that the end state itself is without meaning. Usually the best the mystic can do is to explain the empirical rules and methods which can be used to attain this state. But, since these are empirical means, they are at best empirical interpretations of the abstracted idea and thus cannot contain within them the whole of the abstracted meaning. The end state is not defined by these empirical rules, and this increases the mystic's difficulty of communication.

Since the final aim is abstractive, empirical thought which is not a means to that end is merely a distraction of the individual from his goal. The mystic, therefore, can be expected to retreat from all empirical thought and related empirical concerns not connected to his goal.

3. RELIGIOUS KNOWLEDGE. Religious knowledge combines rational connection of concept to concept with the abstractive connection of concept to observable. The theology consists of connected concepts which are not identical with empirical objects; therefore, religious *thinking* may be wholly rational. Religious *behavior*, however, is abstractive and consists of the attempt to fit the empirical world to nonempirical concepts. Religious concepts, although like most concepts they may have originated as terms identified with empirical objects, are not identified with any empirical objects in the theology.

Theological connections are rational and are made according to logic. These are not loose connections such as those found in magical systems, but are absolute. *Ethical connections* are abstractive and consist of the individual adherence at the observational level to religious laws or ethical rules set up at the theoretic level. Whereas in magical systems rules for action are taken in order to achieve certain empirical ends, ethical rules are obeyed for their own sake.

Religious connections are not attributions of cause which follow from observation of temporal sequences. Cause is theologically a consequence of the action of a conceptualized entity. All conditions and events are effects of the same cause and must be explained with reference to rational concepts. Knowledge in a religious system is of rational connections between concepts and ethical laws. Theological concepts are connected with each other but with nothing else. Ethical concepts are connected with individual actions. The theological connections of concepts must be logically consistent and, since they are connections limited to the theoretic level, cannot be falsified by observable events. The only tests of these connections are direct revelations, mental insights into the connections, and the rules of deductive logic. A logical contradiction between two or more theological connections implies that at least one of them is false within the system, but never that the system as a whole is false. The tests of theology exist only at the theoretic level, and observable events are not relevant to religious truth.

Since they are not falsifiable by observable events, religious connections are regarded as *absolute*. If empirical events are related to theological connections of concepts and appear to contradict them, the system is not thereby false, but instead the events are described as bad, evil, or only apparent and not real. All explanation and prediction of empirical events in religious systems is the result of *interpretation* of theological concepts and therefore is never certain. Worldly things are imperfect, and resulting knowledge may be inexact.

The distinction between *sacred* and *secular* does not apply to magical systems but appears in religious systems. When a society is characterized primarily by a religious system of knowledge, the sacred is defined by the rational religious concepts of the theology. Ordinary activities not related to those concepts constitute the secular domain. In the secular domain empirical connections are made just as in magical systems, but these connections do not deal with questions concerning the nature of the world. Craftsmen and other workers may use their experience and knowledge of observable connections as a basis for actions in relation to production (perhaps in the assurance that god so ordered the world) but successful production has no theological implications. Secular knowledge may be collective in nature and can be learned—a craftsman may teach an apprentice—but, as experience increases, knowledge accumulates and becomes more cumbersome rather than simplified and more easily explanatory. As long as connections are only observable connections, simplifying connections do not exist. Secular knowledge can thus accumulate but never advance.

Sacred knowledge, however, is knowledge pertaining to concepts and their connections. Since these concepts are not limited by specific empirical referents, they may be connected in diverse ways, and the sacred domain may be extended through rational elaboration. Sacred knowledge, as purely theoretic knowledge, may be extended through as many consistent new combinations as it is logically possible to conceive. Religious knowledge may therefore be developmental because of its rational component. While empirical events may cause modifications of empirical connections in the secular domain, the sacred domain is not subject to modification because its theological concepts gain their meaning from their connection to one another and are not connected to observable events.

At times observable events may take forms which have not been perceived before. Such strange or extraordinary events are called *miracles* and are regarded as a separate type of event from the observed empirical phenomena which they appear to contradict.

4. SCIENTIFIC KNOWLEDGE.   Scientific knowledge is based on connections made at both the theoretic and observational levels. Connections of

ideas in scientific systems are therefore both empirical and rational. These two levels are integrated by the third type of connection, abstraction.

All thinking which *combines* rational, empirical, and abstractive thought is scientific. Neither catalogues of empirical facts nor rational systems such as mathematics are scientific thinking by themselves. No system of knowledge is scientific unless it connects the observational and theoretic levels. In the absence of a developed science (as in a religious system of knowledge), technology is representative of empiricist thinking. The development of science implies the integration of such thinking with rationalism through abstraction. Such combination results in the loss of the purely practical orientation of technology and may be distinguished from it in the society in which it occurs; however, in a developed science, theories can always be brought into contact with empirical needs and make technology more effective in meeting them. As the uses of science tend to make a greater impression on individuals, the empirical component may receive more general emphasis, while the abstractive and rational components tend to be accepted as given and true eternally. The rational component may come to be regarded as an empirical statement of the unchanging and ordered nature of things. Therefore, where the technological uses of science are emphasized, scientific revolutions will not be expected. They should occur where application is not stressed at the expense of theory.

When the attempt is made to construct "science" with no more than empirical connection, the result is the same as thinking in a magical system of knowledge. The same or similar rules of connection are used, although methods other than trial and error may be developed as tests of knowledge. Like the results of magical connection, the results of "empirical science" form a catalogue of isolated findings which are not carried to the theoretic level and thus cannot be integrated into an explanatory system. If there is a conception of "theory" in empirical science, it involves the notion that theories are to be *found* (and existing theories were found) by empirical observation.

When the attempt is made to construct "science" with rational connection only, the results are very similar to the results of a religious system. Because it is done in the name of "science," such work is thought to result in "theory." But the use of pure rationalistic connection is more like theology than theory since it lacks empirical application. It may be very complex and inexact, shielding it from contact with the observational level and thus from rejection through disconfirmation. Although it has no value in direct empirical application, rationalistic "science," like any system whose terms have not been rigorously defined for empirical application (and may consequently be very ambiguous), may be comparatively easy to use for explanation after the fact. Like religious dogmas, "scientific rationalistic theories" are promulgated by authority which consequently tends to limit the potential development of new or alternative theories.

It is logically possible to utilize empiricist "science" and "scientific" rationalism, not in combination but in turn, first one and then the other. Explanations may be carried out at the theoretic level while research may involve completely separate fact gathering at the observational level, and no attempt may be made to establish connections between them. This joint, but uncombined, use may give a convincing appearance as "science," but its results will not be similar. Over time, the rational "theory" persists without change, although it may be elaborated, while empirical findings accumulate somewhere else.

The elements of scientific systems are concepts and their referents. Concepts are symbols, not observables. Conceptual meaning cannot be reduced to a set of empirical observations. Instead concepts gain meaning by their relation to other concepts at the theoretic level. They are not identified with their empirical referents but are connected to them through abstraction. Empirical referents may consist simply of conventional empirical categories or they may be measured by formal techniques adapted to facilitate the association of observations with theory.

In scientific systems of knowledge, empirical events are measured at the observational level and are connected through abstraction to concepts at the theoretic level. Empirical objects, regardless of how "real" they are thought to be from a viewpoint outside the scientific system of knowledge, can only enter into the system if some means exists for their measurement. Indeed scientific systems systematically ignore whole classes of attributes of objects for which the means to relate them to theories at the theoretic level have not been developed. Even then, unlike magical systems in which the efficacy of the whole object may be indivisible from its attributes, objects do not enter the scientific system as wholes. Instead only some component or characteristic of the object is subject to the measurement, and the characteristic selected is dictated by the rational concept to which the object is being related.

In a scientific system, connection is equivalent to the isomorphism of observational and theoretic levels. Connections at the theoretic level are hypothetical at the observational level, and neither type of connection is definitive without the other. It is mutual connections which are decisive, rather than rules of thumb or first principles; and these connections must be isomorphic.

Isomorphism of theoretic connections to observational connections implies similarity of structure. Their respective elements (concepts and observationals) are thus connected in similar ways at both levels. But the nature of this similarity is not immediately apparent, for the elements which are connected are quite different. One rational connection might be similar to a variety of empirical connections; therefore, a decisive abstractive association of the two levels must be based upon more than similarity of appearance.

When elaborate empirical relationships are connected through abstraction with a set of isomorphic rational relationships, the collection of related rational relationships is a *theory*. A theory consists of the integration of two or more *laws* or single statements of relationship or connection. This integration involves a rationalization of theoretic connections into a consistent rational system, whereas the empirical categories to which it is connected form a descriptive empirical system. Theory has the same logical character as theology (as well as the same stem). They are both composed of concepts connected rationally at the theoretic level; however, theory has an abstractive isomorphic relationship with the observational level, while theology does not.

Although scientific knowledge may transcend particulars by abstraction from them to an explanatory rational system containing definitionally universal concepts, generalization is not a part of scientific thinking. Generalization is characteristic of simple empiricist thinking and proceeds by a magical rule of thumb, the association of observed particulars with all unobserved or not yet observed particulars believed to be similar. Generalization limits magic to statements of empirical findings and findings projected by association, and therefore will always form a list of bits of information. Science, however, is more efficient because it not only transcends particulars but also provides for the relation of associated concepts in a rational system. The system is a convenience which permits simplified thinking about complex observations.

Unlike magic and mysticism, science has the potential for development. Observed change is not simply added to a body of knowledge but is integrated into and connected with the elements of the rational system. The interplay of the theoretic and observational levels increases the scope of potentiality for developmental change. The two levels tend to build upon each other, increasing the developmental process to greater scope than that found in religion which is limited to rational elaboration.

The test of knowledge in a scientific system is never concerned with empirical or rational connection alone but with the isomorphism of the two. Therefore, the acquisition of knowledge in a scientific system begins with a connection at either the observational or theoretic level. It matters not whether the connection was originally rational or empirical; it does not qualify as scientific knowledge until abstractive connection can be established with the other level. Likewise, tests of isomorphism can be initiated at any time at either level.

A scientific law connecting concepts a and b at the theoretic level with observables A and B, is not automatically rejected if empirical conditions of nonconnection of A and B are once observed. An empirical inconsistency does not "falsify" a law but may simply imply that there are empirical events not yet explained. Laws are accepted for their explanatory and predictive ability, and to speak of falsification implies that the connection between the theoretic and observational levels may have an absolute or true nature independent of the hypothetical abstractive connection; however, this absolute nature contradicts the notion of the acceptance of laws for their relative ability to predict.

The finding of an empirical situation not consistent with a law may, however, simply be evidence of an error in measurement, an incomplete observation, or a lack of observational equipment sufficient to handle the connection expected. Instead of rejecting laws when empirical situations are found which do not appear to be isomorphic, one may seek new techniques and devices for measurement.

CONCEPTIONS OF POWER IN KNOWLEDGE SYSTEMS

Associated with each type of knowledge system and their characteristic types of thought is a distinct conception of power. Magical, mystical, religious, and scientific types of knowledge each possess a unique conception of power which is related to the types of thought used.

1. MAGICAL POWER.   In magical knowledge systems, connections are made exclusively at the observational level. Connections of ideas in magical systems are therefore made only empirically. All activities in a magical system are magical activities based on empirical thinking, and questions of power are not separated from the experiences of daily life. *Power* in a magical system consists of the connection of means to ends, the ability to gain observable results. It is a quantity which is observed in the world and in people; events occur, and that is the result of the power to make them do so. Power is accessible to all, although some individuals may gain or possess more than others. Everyone who acts with any success at all has power. The ability to get from condition A to condition B may be either conceived as an innate characteristic of A (having power as an individual, including individual objects which other knowledge systems usually regard as inanimate) or be demonstrated by some other individual. Power is a characteristic of everything.

Walter B. Miller's description of the Fox Indians provides a good example of this type of power:

> Fox religious thought makes little distinction between the material and non-material, the organic and inorganic, between animal and human, natural and supernatural. All varieties of natural phenomena can gain manitu power by demonstrating qualities or abilities that bring about success in a particular activity.[10]

[10] Walter B. Miller, "Two Concepts of Authority," *American Anthropologist*, Volume 57, 1955, p. 279.

Since power is the ability to attain individual ends, continued success in the world is evidence of an individual's great power while lack of success is evidence of little power. There is no intermediary between power and success. Miller observed of manitu power that

> power is universally available and unlimited; it does not have a unitary locus; it is everywhere, and equally available to all.
>
> The possession of power is temporary and contingent; it is not a quality permanently possessed by any human being, but can be gained and lost, possession being demonstrated by successful performance in specific situations.[11]

An individual not only demonstrates his power in the success of his acts but may possess a distinct subjective feeling of power. The first attainment of this feeling may come with success in some specially signified act, while long term maintenance of the feeling requires continued success in attainment of ends. Power in magical systems may be seen as action in relation to empirical thinking, in relation to knowledge of observed connections.

2. MYSTICAL POWER.   In mystical knowledge systems connections are made both empirically and through abstraction. Empirical connections are made and describe the world as it is, but they do not enter into questions of power. Concern with empirical goals, in fact, is conceived as a way to ensure a lack of power by subordinating the individual to worldly desires. The things of the world are there, they are real, but they do not benefit the individual.

The mystical conception of power is individualistic, as in magic, but it is not empirical. The mystic does not seek worldly ends, but seeks to escape from the powerlessness of the world to an ideal. This ideal is gained by individuals through correct action, and such action consists primarily of devaluating worldly things and pleasures. In this sense magic contradicts mysticism. If one is concerned with power in this world, one cannot escape from it. Religion also conflicts with mysticism in that the mystic is not concerned with the ethical conduct of others or in rational conceptions of the world. All such considerations are a distraction from his goal. Mysticism also clearly conflicts with science. A mystical system of knowledge reflects an individualistic attempt to escape from empiricism and rationalism. It represents a rejection of the prevailing conception of power for an individualistic abstract power.

The successful mystic is the one who is able to lift himself mentally above the concerns of the world. His ultimate aim is to reach in thought some nonempirical state removed from the world. The achievement of this nonworldly mental state is *power* in a mystical system. It is the result of individual action, but not all individuals are able to achieve it, and some do not

---

[11] *Ibid.*, p. 282.

try. Nevertheless, it is not a question of degrees of power in relation to other individuals, as in magical systems, but each individual achievement of mystical power is autonomous. Because it is completely abstractive, mystical power possessed by one individual is not related to the possession of power by another. The abstractive process here is an individualistic phenomenon, not a competitive one.

3. RELIGIOUS POWER.   While it is logically possible for magical systems to encompass the whole of an individual's thought, religious systems of knowledge necessarily apply to a smaller portion. Religious systems deal with questions of power exclusively at the theoretic level. Religious individuals are not thought to possess innate or acquired power; therefore, their day-to-day actions are not dependent upon their system of knowledge and remain at the secularized empirical level. Connections involving power in a religious system originate at the theoretic level.

Power in a religious system is not held by individuals; they conceive of themselves as powerless and all power is thought to reside in a power-concept at the theoretic level. The individual is aware of the operation of power, but he may not possess it or use it himself. Power is not in empirical situations —it is not available in the world. Continued advantages in the world do not follow from correct conduct since power does not result from individual action.

From the point of view of a religious system everyone shares powerlessness in day-to-day actions. At the same time, practical connections can be made at the observational level, but these connections do not relate to individual success or power.

Since a concept such as "God" possesses all the power in a religious conception of the world, individuals having differing success in action cannot attribute it to their own power. It is not power which distinguishes individuals in a religious system, but *authority*, which is simply a position held by virtue of a particular relationship of an individual to the theology. Authority may be gained through knowledge of the theology or through intellectual revelation from the power-concept; but it may not be gained through empirical evidence or success in action. St. Thomas Aquinas described knowledge as sacred doctrine proceeding from *first principles* which are revealed by God. He described the religious authority as the man who knows these first principles. The principles are viewed as accepted on the basis of authority, and the individual who has greater authority may not have more knowledge, but his knowledge is more true—he is closer to God in the authority structure.

An individual in a magical system of knowledge is a causal agent himself and a participant in power. Religion tends to objectify and secularize the world since the individual is at most only an observer of the effects of the power-concept or a carrier of knowledge about the power-concept. All explanations of the action of power in religious systems are to be obtained through authority. If the ordinary man is to base his notions of power and the nature of the world on a religious system, he must have some knowledge of the concepts and connections of the theology; but, beyond learning about his own powerlessness and the powerlessness of the world and the types of ethical behavior relevant to such a world, he is often ignorant of the ramifications of the knowledge of the rational system. This comparative lack of knowledge is of no concern, for his day-to-day actions are mundane by definition, not power related.

For the mystic the idea of power as success in action is rejected for a notion of intellectual escape, but in religion power is still equivalent to success in action, although, it is success which the individual may not share. In this respect religion is the most pessimistic type of knowledge system. There is nothing man may know which is not taught to him by the power-concept, and there is nothing he can accomplish that can be attributed to his own successful action.

4. SCIENTIFIC POWER.   Power in a scientific system of knowledge is the dynamic connection of empirical with rational thinking through abstraction. It is the result of the interplay between observational data and rational calculation and consists of the ability to theoretically anticipate or explain empirical transformations. Power therefore resides neither in the individual nor in the objects of his observation. It appears instead in the interaction of observed empirical connections with mental associations of concepts. Empirical-magical power is accessible to those individuals who are able to use a rational system in relation to the world. But those without knowledge of rational connections and empirical connections or who cannot make connections between them (abstractions) have neither scientific nor magical power. Power is not the ability to gain immediately observable ends. It is neither an individual nor a conceptual phenomenon. Scientific systems demonstrate power in prediction and explanation. Scientific power does not require action by individuals at the observational level (other than the observations themselves). It is not necessarily manipulative. It is in the dynamics of abstraction.

Since theories are postulated a priori and tested a posteriori, they do not merely reflect empirical circumstances. Theory testing never covers the whole range of its implications at the outset. Such a task may take centuries to achieve. The empirical implications of a scientific theory therefore are not limited to what has existed and does exist but extend by rational elaboration to what may not have existed but could exist. Scientific power is not simply the result of the isomorphism of a theory with what is observed, but it extends beyond present empirical knowledge and present empirical conditions to encompass that which could be. Thus, in contrast to empiricism, science is always revolutionary in its implications and may initiate changes because of the necessity contained in its rationalism. On the other hand, science has been under the control of nonscientific systems of knowledge throughout its history. In the United States, science has been successfully controlled by the empiricist power of politicians and propertied classes and has been primarily directed toward empiricist ends, in spite of its own implications. This may partially explain the concentration of scientific development in physical knowledge while the social sciences remain at an empiricist prescientific level. Scientific power remains separate from social action.

What scientific power is, is well expressed in the frequently heard comment that a theory is powerful. To say that a theory is powerful is to note that it can be used to explain and predict empirical events. Galileo's theory of falling bodies was more powerful than Aristotle's because its predictions and explanations were more accurate when applied to empirical circumstances. Einstein's theory was more useful than Newton's in crucial circumstances and is considered more powerful. It can be seen that power is determined by the scope of application of the theory as well as the accuracy, although scope and accuracy are connected. The theory which is accurate for a wider range of phenomena is the more powerful.

The use of theory by empirical thinkers as if it were an empirical "discovery" may also produce magical power. A theory may be used to make empirical changes for empirical ends and thus to produce what is essentially magical power in a more complex society. Theory may form the basis for producing more efficient weapons to subdue greater numbers of people, an empirical end which has not been determined in any way by scientific thinking.

On the other hand, there are scientific theories which have power in explaining empirical phenomena but which cannot (at least not presently) be used to influence changes. We may know quite well how to change the orbit of Mars because we can explain its operation theoretically, but we may not have the empirical means to do it. Similarly, if scientific social knowledge were developed, it might point out the conditions under which a society free from suffering and want could exist, but the means necessary for that transformation probably would not lie in the hands of the scientist himself.

Since empirical thinking is an integral part of science, it can never retreat from "worldly affairs" as can religion and mysticism. Since rational thinking is an integral part of science, it cannot pursue empirical ends alone as can magic. The rationality of science is impersonal, and its explanatory power is individual. By combining the three types of thinking, science may cover more scope than the other types of knowledge systems.

CHAPTER FOUR

THE MAGICAL KNOWLEDGE OF THE AZANDE

Magical knowledge based on the use of empirical thinking in conjunction with the notion of individual personal power is characteristic of primitive societies. A primitive society here refers to a small, relatively isolated, society in which there is no clear division of mental from manual labor, no organization of groups of individuals into classes according to specialized social interests, and no development of a written system of symbols. This does not mean that there will be no mental labor but that the mental laborer will not subsist on that labor alone. Mental laborers, likewise, will not be numerous enough to form an organized class of people, although there may be associations of these individuals if they have served an apprenticeship in the particular type of mental skill represented. Such a group is necessarily too small to influence the existing social organization. Only if many such groups form one larger group would one be able to designate them as a class organization, and when a society has reached that state it is already too large to be referred to as a primitive society.

Primitive society, as it has been described, is characterized by magical knowledge. Magical knowledge relies upon empirical thought, the only type of thought possible in a society without the mental skills, specialties, and symbolism necessary to develop a rational system of ideas. On the basis of size alone, there is no possibility of a complex division of labor necessary for the development of a rational system. As the society is simple, its thought is simple, and its knowledge consists of a catalogue of means for achieving ends (magical power) arrived at by the association of empirical observations.

The only goals in primitive society are empirical ones arising from day-to-day associations and basic human needs.

In a primitive society all knowledge is magical. The modern notion of magical knowledge is just that, a modern notion. To the primitive no other kind of knowledge exists. All thought is empirical, all action is power related, and thus all knowledge is magical. His knowledge is magical both when it appears so to the nonprimitive observer, as when he participates in witchcraft, and when it seems to be associated with the mundane, as when he explains why he constructs implements in a certain way. Only in more complex societies, and then only after the development of either religion or some form of rationalism, is magic a special type of knowledge.

In this work, *magic* is being used in a special sense. It has been defined in order that its existence as a type of knowledge system can be definitely and unquestionably distinguished from religious, mystic, and scientific systems in any empirical case. Although it is a type of thinking expected to be characteristic of the most primitive cultures, the spread of Western civilization has reduced the possibility that such hypothetically possible "pure" cases can be found for study.

The Zande culture of central Africa studied by Evans-Pritchard is not such a pure case (since it has not remained isolated) and therefore cannot be expected always to conform to the features of a magical system of knowledge. The Azande had been influenced at the time Evans-Pritchard studied them both by frequent contact with Western civilization and by contact with other (possibly more advanced) African cultures. In addition the territory of influence of Zande culture itself was not limited to a small isolated tribe but was widespread and consisted of a number of "kingdoms." In spite of these variations from the ideal conditions for studying magical systems, the conditions are close enough that a magical system of knowledge should be expected to predominate.[1]

Evans-Pritchard's terms are different from (but not contradictory to) those used here. He distinguished empirical categories of *witchcraft, magic* (and its subcategory *leechcraft*), and *sorcery*. *Witchcraft* is the use of power of the mind to influence or cause injury to persons or property. The man who is a witch is so by birth, having been born with an observable witchcraft substance in his body.[2] I am taking the liberty of relabeling Evans-Pritchard's category of "magic" as *witch-doctoring* in order to eliminate any confusion between his term and my use of "magic" to refer to a type of system of knowledge. Witch-doctoring then is the use of power through knowledge or

---

[1] In other words, they conform rather closely to the description of a primitive society.

[2] See E.E. Evans-Pritchard, *Witchcraft, Oracles and Magic Among the Azande* (Oxford: Oxford University Press, 1937), pp. 9–10. This, and following excerpts from *Witchcraft*, are reprinted by permission of the Clarendon Press, Oxford.

skill, taking the form of the use of medicines or drugs. *Leechcraft* is surgery to treat pathological conditions. *Sorcery* is the illicit or destructive use of medicine or drugs.[3]

Evans-Pritchard used a number of other terms which will not be necessary here and thus are not elaborated. The free use and combination of terms is consistent with empirical description. As Evans-Pritchard himself indicated, "If the labels do not prove helpful we can discard them. The facts will be the same without the labels."[4] It is his ability to report the facts, regardless of their labels, which makes his work so helpful.

Since Zande social conditions approximate those of primitive societies outlined above, all Zande thought should be empirical, all actions should be means toward empirical ends (power related), and all knowledge should be magical. The empirical categories described by Evans-Pritchard should therefore be inseparable from other observable activities as means for getting from condition A to condition B.

But Evans-Pritchard has indicated that he believes that a certain element of Zande culture is *mystical*, involving "patterns of thought that attribute to phenomena supra-sensible qualities which, or part of which, are not derived from observation or cannot be logically inferred from it, and which they do not possess."[5] This assertion may be regarded as one test of the theory of systems of knowledge. If the Azande themselves have attained advanced elements of a religious or mystic system of knowledge (including the notion that power is not held by individuals) or if they have imposed elements of a different type of system of knowledge on their own magical system, such mystical notions might be expected. But if the Azande believe that power is only in observable individuals, if they have not adopted pieces of a foreign system of knowledge, those "mystical" notions will in fact be simple empiricist thinking which gives a superficial appearance of being connected to the theoretic level because their content is similar to that of the religious or mystic systems of knowledge with which we, the observers, are more familiar. Here, as in other circumstances, the test of empiricist thinking is whether it connects observable directly to observable, no matter how strange the connection may appear to an outside mind.

Evans-Pritchard's study of the Azande should indicate the isomorphism of the theory of magical systems of knowledge with empirical events occurring under conditions close to those of primitive society. The analysis will proceed by presenting the basic features of Zande thinking and action, as

---

[3] Evans-Pritchard's terms were defined as empirical categories, and it therefore does not violate scientific procedure to relabel them when another term will make the exposition more clear.

[4] *Ibid.*, p. 11.

[5] *Ibid.*, p. 12.

Evans-Pritchard described them, and will indicate how those features are or are not isomorphic to the theory.

For the Azande, witchcraft results from the presence in the body of a certain substance.[6] This substance (observed after death and found in the abdomen of the corpse by autopsy) is inherited and transmitted directly from parent to child. The sons of male witches are witches, and the daughters of female witches are witches; but witchcraft substance is not inherited across sexes. The notion of the sex-linked inheritance of witchcraft substance follows from the notion that conception of a male child takes place when the father's "soul" is stronger than the mother's, while a female child is the result of the strength of the mother's soul. Thus (thinking empirically) male (or female) witchcraft substance is inherited with other male (or female) characteristics from the father (or mother) because of stronger influence of one parent.

Evans-Pritchard points out that this belief, when carried to its rational conclusion, implies that all the members of a man's clan should be witches if he is a witch since the Zande clan consists of individuals biologically related through the male line. But he found that in actual practice only the close relatives of a known witch are regarded as witches. In fact, "A Zande is interested in witchcraft only as an agent on definite occasions and in relation to his own interests, and not as a permanent condition of individuals."[7] In immediate situations a man may claim not to be related to a witch in his clan by claiming the witch to be a bastard. The possession of witchcraft by the female does not, of course, reflect on the clan which is made up of male kin.

Evans-Pritchard points to what he perceives as a contradiction between the hereditary sex-linked transmission of witchcraft and the notion that only the close kin of a known witch are regarded as witches; but this lack of tracing of the logical implications of empirical generalizations should be characteristic of magical systems of knowledge. The connection of observable to observable may be directly related to an empirical generalization ("all sons of witches are witches") but any further implications may not be carried out. It is the immediate empirical circumstance which is relevant, not possible, nonobservable, or potential (or even past) circumstances. It is therefore consistent that the Azande do not attribute this to individuals as a "permanent condition," although in the abstract sense and if thought out to a rational conclusion, it might be expected. If the circumstance which called up the attribution of witchcraft is past, the attribution has no empirical relevance to the Azande and is forgotten.

The Azande regard death as a direct consequence of the psychic action

---

[6] The description that follows is taken from *ibid.*, Chapter I, pp. 21–39.
[7] *Ibid.*, p. 26.

of witches. Death must always be avenged, but "As soon as a witch is to-day slain by magic, or in the past had been speared to death or had paid compensation, the affair is closed."[8] The implications of the Zande attitude toward death and vengence are twofold when considered in the context of magical culture. To an empirical thinker in a magical system of knowledge, every act is a power act—every new event is the result of the action of power by some individual; therefore, the death of a man must have been caused by psychic action which they know (by the experience of their own minds) exists but which they cannot see in others. The explanation is a connection of the observable event to an immediate cause which has been previously observed even though it may not have been directly experienced in this case. To the magical thinker, this explanation is the only one possible—death must have been at the hand of another man (since individuals cause all events) and the operation of the murderer's psyche provides the simplest empirical answer. Witches, then, cause death by means of psychic power. The immediate closing of concern about the death as soon as vengence has been taken is consistent with the empiricist concern with the immediately observable.

Witchcraft substance grows with the aging of the body, and an old witch is regarded as more powerful than a young one. It follows that children will not possess much witchcraft substance and thus will not be accused of murder since they do not have the power needed to carry it off.[9] Children know about witches; in fact, everyone is an authority on the subject. Male witches are sought as causes of misfortune to males and female witches are connected with female misfortune. Zande witchcraft conforms to the expectations of the theory of a magical system of knowledge in that it has qualities associated with it which are identical to those observed in living things. Not only does witchcraft substance grow as the body grows, but it has a psychic component as does the body. Its character is so straightforward and non-mysterious that even the children know of it and understand it. Witchcraft is connected to observable qualities as well. It is a perceived aspect of daily experience. It is defined according to its empirical manifestations, as are all elements of a magical system.

The empirical basis of witchcraft (in spite of superficial appearances to Western observers) is indicated most strongly by the ultimate test of its existence—the autopsy. Only this direct empirical evidence of the existence or nonexistence of witchcraft substance in a body after death can finally confirm that a man (or woman) is or is not a witch.

The notion of the psychic nature of the action of witchcraft requires additional consideration since it is not immediately evident that this notion

[8] *Ibid.*, p. 27.
[9] See *ibid.*, p. 30.

can be solely empirical in its origin. Evans-Pritchard seems to have been somewhat confused by the fact that the word for the soul of a man and the word for the psychic part of witchcraft were the same. But this does not appear confusing in the larger picture of what the "soul" must mean to an empiricist in a magical system. The individual *observes* that he himself has both body and soul (mind). He *observes* that his soul is frequently active when his body is at rest (in dreams). He likewise *observes* that there are times when the soul appears to leave the body completely (at death). A certain autonomy of the soul is implied by observation. To explain death (the removal of the soul from the body) it seems clear that some action must have been taken upon that soul by some other soul (since souls have been observed to effect other souls in dreams, but bodies do not appear to be able to effect souls). This action was clearly taken by a more powerful soul (meaning one that is more effective in action), and its possessor is known as a "witch." Thus the notion of witches as individuals having a hereditary substance making their souls more powerful than ordinary souls is empirical in character. An empirical event must have a direct cause in individual action, and the notion of a witch as an individual with a more powerful soul who occasionally uses it to destroy other souls is the obvious explanation on the basis of observation alone. It is not confusing, therefore, that the word for soul is the same in both instances; it is likely that the distinction made by Evans-Pritchard amounts to no more than different manifestations of the same thing. Witches, it must be remembered, are not strange otherworldly beings having mysterious ways; they take part in everyday life and should be expected to have souls like everyone else. Empirical cases of individuals wishing others harm followed by the actual occasion of harm is frequent enough to be the basis for empirical generalization.[10]

This explanation which would have been expected from considering the observable features of the soul in sleep and death conforms to Evans-Pritchard's description: "Azande generally think of a witch sending his soul on errands by night when his victim is asleep."[11] Action of soul on soul, a psychic event, is usually put in the observable context of soul action—sleep.[12]

Tylor's notion of the "materiality" of the soul in primitive conceptions, as opposed to the idea of an immaterial soul, seems to bear out the magical-empirical interpretation favored here. Significantly, he noted that "The act of breathing, so characteristic of the higher animals during life, and coinciding so closely with life in its departure, has been repeatedly and naturally

---

[10] The English term "soul" itself probably has an empirical source since its original meaning was "breath." The folk idea that one should say, "God bless you," when someone else sneezes, though framed in religious terms, rests on the notion that the soul is sneezed out of the body, leaving it momentarily powerless, a clearly magical and empirical idea.

[11] *Ibid.*, p. 33.

[12] See *ibid,*. p. 136.

identified with the life or soul itself."[13] The repeated observation of this coincidence in conjunction with the experience of encountering other individuals, dead or alive, in dreams must represent convincing empirical evidence that man is composed of a body and a separate "material" soul, and that death consists of the separation of the two. Tylor noted conceptions of the soul very like that of the Azande among the North American Indians, the New Zealanders, the Greenlanders, and others.[14]

The Azande also attribute witchcraft powers to various animals although Evans-Pritchard states that he is unable to determine to what extent they take them seriously. It is probable that they do not always take the matter seriously, but the descriptions of experiences related to the powers of animals and specific "spells" relating to animals makes it appear that they once did consider it quite seriously. The theory of the magical system of knowledge indicates that in a pure case one can expect the attribution of power (and will) to all individuals as parts of a web of power relations including plants, animals, men, and inanimate objects, a condition from which the Azande have developed.

"Witchcraft is ubiquitous. It plays its part in every activity of Zande life; in agricultural, fishing, and hunting pursuits; in domestic life ... court ... oracles and magic ... law and morals ... technology and language; there is no niche or corner of Zande culture into which it does not twist itself."[15] In other words, it provides an immediate empirical category to connect with any unfortunate event: "Witchcraft is a classification of misfortunes which while differing from each other in other respects have this single common character, their harmfulness to man."[16]

Witchcraft provides an explanation for particular events. The questions answered in magical systems of knowledge are not questions of ultimates, questions of abstract relations, or questions of scientific law, and the Azande were not found to be concerned with that type of question:

> Why, then, should this particular man on this one occasion in a life crowded with similar situations in which he and his friends emerged scatheless have been gored by this particular beast? Why he and not someone else? Why on this occasion and not on other occasions? Why by this elephant and not by other elephants? It is the particular and variable conditions of an event and not the general and universal conditions that witchcraft explains. Fire is hot, but

[13] Sir Edward Burnett Tylor, *Religion in Primitive Culture* (New York: Harper & Brothers Publishers, 1958), p. 16.

[14] See *ibid.*, pp. 16–18. Spiro also noted a similar conception among the Burmese. See Melford E. Spiro, *Burmese Supernaturalism* (Englewood Cliffs: Prentice-Hall, Inc., 1967), p. 69. Frazer referred to several instances, See Sir James G. Frazer, *The Golden Bough: A Study in Magic and Religion*, abridged edition (New York: the Macmillan Company, 1958), pp. 208–25.

[15] Evans-Pritchard, *Witchcraft*, p. 63.

[16] *Ibid.*, p. 64.

it is not hot owing to witchcraft, for that is its nature. It is a universal quality of fire to burn, but it is not a universal quality of fire to burn *you*.[17]

This type of explanation may be explained by the theory of magical knowledge in that it is concerned with the connection of particular to particular. Zande explanation provides an extra *why* for any event, a *why* which modern Western civilization (not concerned with power relations in *every* event) attributes to chance. In a magical system of knowledge, however, nothing happens without having been caused to do so; nothing happens which is not a manifestation of power.

Evans-Pritchard claims that "witchcraft has its own logic, its own rules of thought," but this is a result of comprehending witchcraft from a foreign point of view. Western observers do not conceive of witchcraft as a causal agent; therefore, it must be a special sort of concept. But to the Azande it is clear that witchcraft is that causal agent which leads to the misfortunes an individual does not cause himself. Laziness, incompetence, ignorance, and carelessness may all be causes of misfortune. From the Zande point view it would not change the quality of that list of causes to add witchcraft to it. In fact: "Belief in witchcraft is quite consistent with human responsibility and a rational appreciation of nature."[18] Viewing magic as empirical eliminates the necessity of creating a new logic for its understanding and makes it consistent within the limits of empirical thought. The Azande are neither nonrational nor irrational unless the observer projects his own culture bound categories to their thought.

Evans-Pritchard poses the question of whether the Azande distinguish causation by witchcraft from other types of causation. It would be consistent with the theory of magical knowledge that they do not. Evans-Pritchard, however, claims that it is different because it "transcends sensory experience;"[19] but that distinction is *his*—empirical perception can no more distinguish between "sensory" experience and "nonsensory" experience than between the "natural" and the "supernatural." Evans-Pritchard's own reporting is comprehensive enough to make it quite clear that they do not make the latter distinction:

> To us supernatural means very much the same as abnormal or extraordinary. Azande certainly have no such notions of reality. They have no conception of 'natural' as we understand it, and therefore neither of the 'supernatural' as we understand it. What we call supernatural we raise to a different plane, even thought of spacially, from the plane of the natural. But witchcraft is to Azande an ordinary and not an extraordinary, even though it may in

[17] *Ibid.*, p. 69.
[18] *Ibid.*, p. 79.
[19] *Ibid.*, p. 81.

some circumstances be an infrequent, event. It is a normal, and not an abnormal, happening.[20]

If the Azande do distinguish differences between witchcraft and other causes as Evans-Pritchard claims, it appears that this distinction is only of one kind of cause from another, having no more significance than a distinction between other causes such as carelessness, ignorance, and incompetence. The observation that the Azande are unable to discuss the implications of witchcraft is an indication that this type of question has no relevance to them—is outside their system of knowledge which is nevertheless reasonable for those who think only empirically. Abstraction does not appear to have any meaning for them. Evans-Pritchard observed:

> In truth Azande experience feelings about witchcraft rather than ideas, for their intellectual concepts of it are weak and they know better what to do when attacked by it than how to explain it.[21]

In short, the Azande are empirical thinkers and have no abstract concepts: witchcraft "is less an intellectual symbol than a response to situations of failure."[22]

Witchcraft also exemplifies the Zande notion of power. After a death the witch who caused it is sought among the dead man's enemies, those who have threatened him, and those who have exhibited offensive behavior.[23] These, of course, are empirical criteria by which to identify a man who may have done harm. However:

> Those whom we would call good citizens—and, of course, the richer and more powerful members of society are such—are seldom accused of witchcraft, while those who make themselves a nuisance to their neighbors and those who are weak are most likely to be accused of witchcraft.[24]

Power for good results in observable gain while power for bad results in observable loss (or death). Evans-Pritchard attributes this discrepancy between rich and poor in accusations of witchcraft to the fear of retaliation by the rich if they are accused.[25] This, too, is consistent with an empirical orientation. Thus, the Azande have notions of power resulting in accumulation of good and power from ability to do harm. The power of witches is nicely illustrated in the following story:

[20] *Ibid.*, pp. 80–81.
[21] *Ibid.*, p. 82.
[22] *Ibid.*, p. 83.
[23] See *ibid.*, pp. 107–9.
[24] *Ibid.*, p. 112.
[25] See *ibid.*, p. 113.

> Tupoi had a great failing for beer and invariably seemed to get news when I intended to give a pot or two to my retainers and neighbors, and, though uninvited, he would as invariably make his appearance at the party. I found this so annoying that I strictly forbad beer to be given to him. I was not obeyed, and on inquiry I was told that no one was prepared to take the risk of passing round a gourd and leaving Tupoi out, since he was undoubtedly a witch and would harm any one who so insulted him.[26]

Tupoi obviously had more power than Evans-Pritchard—power attributed to him because of his reputation for ability in action.

To Evans-Pritchard, looking at the Azande from a rational-empirical point of view, their notion of witchcraft is contradictory because, although they are convinced that others are guilty, they never admit that they are themselves witches.[27] But he says that he believes "witchcraft is imaginary;"[28] however, at the same time he claims it "is a response to certain situations and not an intricate intellectual concept."[29] What he apparently does not see is that the contradiction is in his own rational conception of witchcraft as imaginary while maintaining an empirical conception of witchcraft as a response to situations. The Azande are not contradicting themselves when they point to the evidence of witchcraft but never admit to being witches themselves—both are consistent with their sense perceptions. Evans-Pritchard explains how this "contradiction" is resolved: "An individual experience when it contradicts accepted opinion does not prove accepted opinion to be untrue, but merely that the individual experience is peculiar and inadequate."[30] But the contradiction is in his own mind. Only if the Azande made the empirical generalization that *all* men are witches while each denied being a witch would there be any contradiction in empirical thinking.

The Azande seem to have faith in witch-doctoring in exactly the same way that many modern Westerners have faith in medical doctors—depending on the success of their actions (or power in a magical system of knowledge). This faith relative to power tends to maintain the practice of witchdoctoring: "Scepticism explains failures of witch-doctors, and being directed toward particular witch-doctors even tends to support faith in others."[31]

Specialists in the use of skills and empirical knowledge (such as drugs and medicines) in a magical system of knowledge are expected to be trained through apprenticeship; but, since power relationships do not imply authority relationships, there should not be differences of status based on anything

---

[26] *Ibid.*, p. 116.
[27] See *ibid.*, p. 119.
[28] *Ibid.*, p. 119.
[29] *Ibid.*, p. 118.
[30] *Ibid.*, p. 120.
[31] *Ibid.*, p. 193.

but success in practice. This is true of Zande witch-doctoring: it was observed that "leadership among witch-doctors is never institutional, and that there is an entire absence of grades based on seniority. Each witch-doctor acts on his own account, has his own practice, collects his own fees, and, generally speaking, is responsible to no one but himself in matters pertaining to professional conduct. His diploma consists in his knowledge of certain medicines which he has learnt from another witch-doctor."[32]

Witch-doctoring, like witchcraft, is an empirical practice. It is the use of observable means to observable ends: "the Zande does not believe in the therapeutic powers of witch-doctors through a special ability to believe in things supernatural . . . he always refers your scepticism to the test of experience."[33] The treatment of ills through witch-doctoring is an empirical action. It has empirically observable successes and failures, and the Azande are able to tell a good witch-doctor from a quack by his competence in doing the proper things to effect cures. The nature of witch-doctoring is best exemplified by Evans-Pritchard's observations:

> If you accompany a witch-doctor on one of his visits you will be convinced, if not of the validity of his cures, at least of his skill. As far as you can observe, everything which he does appears to be aboveboard, and you will notice nothing which might help you to detect a fraud. When you have lived for some time in Zandeland you will also have ample evidence of the therapeutic value of the kind of treatment which witch-doctors employ. Every native can give you from his own experience convincing accounts of how he and his relatives and friends have been cured by the extraction of bones or worms from their bodies. If one witch-doctor fails to cure a Zande he goes to another in the same way as we go to another doctor if we are dissatisfied with the treatment of the first one whom we have consulted. Thus Kamanga, before he was initiated into the craft himself, was ill for some weeks. He first went to a witch-doctor who extracted all sorts of little objects without making him any better because, so Kamanga said, he had inefficiently left some of these shafts of witchcraft still embedded in his body. He appears to have visited other specialists before consulting Badobo, who told him that he was very ill and, if not treated at once, he would die. The other witch-doctors whom he had previously consulted had diagnosed his illness as pneumonia and a variety of other ills, whereas Badobo said that it was *ima wangu*, and he gave him *mbiro* medicine to eat and massaged him, and produced two bones out of his body, and sent him home to lie down and get some sleep. Kamanga, however, became worse and worse as the day went on and suffered considerable pain. He had heard in the past that a woman witch-doctor who lived nearby had a reputation for honesty and skill, so he decided to pay her a visit the same evening. She said that she would help him, and when he had given her half a piastre she prepared a *kpoyo* poultice and felt his belly. 'Good gracious,' she said, 'you are troubled with worms.' She proceeded to extract them by first placing the poultice on his body and then, after it had rested there for a short while, by sucking his belly with her

[32] *Ibid.*, p. 202.
[33] *Ibid.*, p. 232.

mouth. She sucked from his body seven worms, and Kamanga went home feeling much better. His belly was cooler, and the pain had left him. In three days he was quite well again.[34]

This story probably sounds familiar to the patients of many modern medical doctors, even frighteningly familiar because, when the competence of a doctor is judged only empirically by his results, the patient has no alternative other than to keep shopping around until he is able to get the results he hoped for. In fact, M.D.s typically have no understanding of exactly how their drugs and medications work. They only know that the drug company says that they work and that when they are used they often have the desired result. The M.D. is clearly not very different from his primitive forebear, the witch-doctor.

The Azande seek the services of witch-doctors if they want quick answers, but the poison oracle is regarded as more dependable.[35] Poison provides an unquestionable empirical test—either the victim (in this case a fowl) dies, behaves strangely, or does not die; and these actions mean specific things. As the test of the fowl can be related to all events or actions, it can be used to judge not only past situations but to indicate the success of future actions. The poison oracle is all-important because his answers are not subject to human error but depend decisively on empirical test.

According to Evans-Pritchard, the poison oracle tells a Zande "his enemies, tells him where he may seek safety from danger, shows him hidden mystic forces, and describes past and future."[36] Here again he has used the term "mystic," but I am unable to discover what it refers to. The list of events about which the poison oracle is frequently consulted seems extremely nonmystical and very empirical-practical:

> To discover why a wife has not conceived.
> During pregnancy of a wife, about place of delivery, about her safety in child-birth, and the safety of her child.
> Before circumcision of a son.
> Before marriage of a daughter.
> Before sending son to act as page at court.
> In sickenss of any member of family. Will he die? Who is the witch responsible? &c.
> To discover the agent responsible for any misfortune.
> At death of kinsman in the old days. Who killed him? Who will execute the witch? &c.
> Before exacting vengeance by magic. Who will keep the taboos? Who will make the magic? &c.
> In cases of sorcery.

---

[34] *Ibid.*, pp. 232–33.
[35] See *ibid.*, p. 258.
[36] *Ibid.*, p. 263.

In cases of adultery.
Before gathering oracle poison.
Before making blood-brotherhood.
Before long journeys.
A man before marrying a wife.
Before large-scale hunting.
A commoner choosing a new homestead site.
Before accepting, or allowing a dependent to accept, European employment.
Before becoming a witch-doctor.
Before joining a closed association.
A man before he and his adult sons go to war.
In cases of disloyalty to a prince.
A prince before making war.
To determine disposition of warriors, place and time of attack, and all other matters pertaining to warfare.
A prince before appointing governors, deputies, or any other officials.
A prince before moving his court.
A prince to discover whether a communal ceremony will terminate drought.
A prince to determine the actions of the British District Commissioner.
A prince before accepting presents and tribute.[37]

In short, the Azande consult the poison oracle on empirical grounds only, relating to any case of action whether past or projected.

In actuality, Evans-Pritchard seems not to mean "nonempirical" by the term "mystic" but "hidden" which is significantly different in implication to the Western observer. He points out that, to the Azande, witchcraft is similar to adultery in that both are subjects about which to consult the poison oracle because they are not *seen*.[38] But to call this "mystical" or "nonempirical" tends to ignore the fact that empiricists may use empirical data both inductively and deductively. A sufficient amount of empirical data may lead to an inductive knowledge (or suspicion) that is itself purely empirical and not at all mystical. Both witchcraft and adultery are definite acts, the effects of which are quite clear—neither is a mystical concept.

The poison oracle is in the fowl and reveals itself with the reaction of the bird. The answer given is dependent on the question but is empirically decisive, as in the following examples.

A

First Test. If X has committed adultery poison oracle kill the fowl. If X is innocent poison oracle spare the fowl. The fowl dies.
Second Test. The poison oracle has declared X guilty of adultery by slaying the fowl. If its declaration is true let it spare this second fowl. The fowl survives.
Result. A valid verdict. X is guilty.

---

[37] *Ibid.*, pp. 261–62.
[38] See *ibid.*, p. 269.

B

First Test. If X has committed adultery poison oracle kill the fowl. If X is innocent poison oracle spare the fowl. The fowl lives.
Second Test. The poison oracle has declared X innocent of adultery by sparing the fowl. If its declaration is true let it slay the second fowl. The fowl dies.
Result. A valid verdict. X is innocent.

C

First Test. If X has committed adultery poison oracle kill the fowl. If X is innocent poison oracle spare the fowl. The fowl dies.
Second Test. The poison oracle has declared X guilty of adultery by slaying the fowl. If its declaration is true let it spare the second fowl. The fowl dies.
Result. The verdict is contradictory and therefore invalid.[39]

If the results are indecisive the poison oracle must be consulted again at a different occasion.[40]

If consulted at two different times about the future, the verdict of the poison oracle may appear to change from one time to another, but in reality it is the future conditions which have changed:

> I have often noticed that Azande on being informed that sickness lies ahead of them do not even proceed to discover the name of the witch whose influence is going to cause them sickness and get him to blow out water but merely wait for a few days and then consult the oracle again to find out whether their health will be good for the coming month, hoping that by the time of the second consultation the evil influence which hung over their future at the time of the first consultation will no longer be there. As a man's future is dependent upon the oracle he does not need to look further than the oracle for his future is contained in the oracle and caused by it. Azande do not, of course, see the matter in this light. To them there is a real change in future conditions. To us there is only a change in the verdict of the oracle.
>
> It follows that present and future have not entirely the same meaning for Azande as they have for us. Time has a different value. It is difficult to formulate the problem in our language, but it would appear from their behavior (I am not speaking of expressed patterns of thought) that the present and future overlap in some way so that the present partakes of the future as it were. Hence a man's future health and happiness depend on future conditions that are already in existence and can be exposed by the oracles and altered. The future depends on the disposition of mystical forces that can be tackled here and now. Moreover, when the oracles announce that a man will fall sick, i.e., be bewitched in the near future, his 'condition' is therefore already bad, his future is already part of him. Azande cannot explain these matters, they content themselves with believing and enacting them.[41]

This has particular significance for the predictable empirical percep-

---

[39] *Ibid.*, p. 300.
[40] Apparently the test used to be even more decisive, and people once occasionally drank the oracle poison themselves.
[41] *Ibid.*, pp. 346–47. It is obvious that "mystical" could here again be interpreted as "hidden."

tion of time which appears in it. As time is not an abstract continuum to the Azande as it is to Evans-Pritchard, it is clear that future conditions may be "already in existence" yet may be altered by present actions. The use of the "afterwards therefore because of" empirical association is relevant to all events, no matter if they are perceived by others as being on an abstract unalterable time continuum. Evans-Pritchard's statement that "these things are felt rather than formulated, for to formulate clearly beliefs such as those recounted in the last few paragraphs would be to expose their hollowness"[42] exposes instead the misunderstanding to be gained from trying to impose an abstraction on an empiricist notion of time.

The attitudes (and so-called mysticism) of the Azande toward sorcery, medicines used to produce harmful effects, are very similar to those of witchcraft and need not be discussed at length. Sorcery, like witchcraft, is hidden; no one admits to practicing it. But, unlike witchcraft, it employs medicines to effect this misfortune. Just as witchcraft and witch-doctoring are consistent with a magical system of knowledge, sorcery is also since it shares their characteristics, and the attitudes toward it are the same. Specific Zande medicines are used for specific purposes just as are any medicines. They are empirical techniques used for the empirical effects they produce.

In his discussion of leechcraft Evans-Pritchard takes up the question of the nonempirical in greater detail.

> Is Zande leechcraft in any degree empirically sound, or is it pure magic? Let us frame this question clearly. When we describe some economic activity we sometimes find that it comprises two types of customary behavior, the empirical and the ritual. We differentiate between these two types of behavior by their objective results and by the quality of the notions associated with them. When a man hoes his garden and plants eleusine it is an empirical performance because it has the result aimed at and because no mystical notions are adduced to explain it; whereas when he squeezes a liquid (which is not a manure) on the eleusine plants to make them grow and multiply it is a ritual performance because it does not produce the result aimed at and because the action is explained mystically by reference to witchcraft and magic. When a man digs a hole to trap animals he acts empirically and explains his behavior in a common-sense way; but when, having dug the hole, he strips naked and jumps over it, we do not regard his action as empirical because it in no way affects the movement of animals as it is believed to do. When a man chooses a suitable tree and fells it and hollows its wood into a gong his actions are empirical, but when he abstains from sexual intercourse during his labour we speak of his abstinence as ritual, since it has no objective relation to the making of gongs and since it involves ideas of taboo. We thus classify Zande behavior into empirical and ritual, and Zande notions into common sense and mystical, according to our knowledge of natural processes and not according to theirs. For we raise quite a different question when we ask whether the Zande himself distinguishes between those techniques we call empirical and those techniques we call magical.[43]

---

[42] *Ibid.*, p. 347.
[43] *Ibid.*, p. 492.

Evans-Pritchard's distinction between the magical and the empirical is of great significance to the validity of this theory. If the magical is non-empirical to the Azande or if the Zande system of knowledge exhibits nonempirical features, then the theory is wrong. But it is quite clear that Evans-Pritchard is not saying that the Zande *way of thinking* is anything but empirical but that their *behavior* is nonempirical from *his own way of thinking*. Indeed, the empirical-ritual distinction is each time explicitly introduced as a conception of the outside observer. Without a theory of systems of knowledge with which to understand foreign systems, it is impossible to avoid categorizing those systems in terms of the system of knowledge of the outside observer. Doing so involves the outside observer in the perception of contradictions which, it seems quite clear from the analysis presented here, do not exist when the Azande are perceived as thinking in empirical terms alone. The contradictions and unanswered questions raised by Evans-Pritchard appear to be a result of trying to understand Zande thinking in rational-empirical terms.

If the Azande themselves perceived a difference between the empirical and the nonempirical and thus acted with more or less conviction on the basis of the two types of thinking, the existence of the nonempirical would be decisive. But this certainly is not the case. The Azande think empirically in relation to all their actions:

> In what, then, lies the difference between the magical and the empirical elements in Zande leechcraft? The Zande himself does not see any qualitative difference, and it is we who classify his leechcraft into two and mutually exclusive categories. We must therefore frame our question in other terms: What difference can we observe between the behavior of Azande when they are using drugs which are of real therapeutic value and their behavior when they are using drugs of no therapeutic value? The man who sucked the snake-bite and gave the bitten boy drugs to eat clearly considered both actions necessary. A man who places a basket over his maternal uncle's head and pours cold water over him to cure early morning nausea does not distinguish the therapeutic effect of his actions from those of a man who smears honey over a scalded skin. If witchcraft does not interfere, both treatments will be efficacious. But can we perceive any difference between the one kind of behavior and the other that would justify us in regarding them as distinct types with well-defined contrasting characteristics?
>
> I think not. [44] . . . Nor can we differentiate magical behavior by reference to the emotional states of performers.[45]

The empirical behavior of sucking snake-bites to remove venom has been characteristic of many societies. It appears to be the correct empirical behavior to produce the effect of removing the venom. But if our medical doctors claimed that this action produces the opposite effect, we would

[44] *Ibid.*, p. 504.
[45] *Ibid.*, p. 505.

believe it and think that giving the boy drugs was the more effective procedure. Thus it is clearly perception by the outsider that makes one of these actions empirical and the other non-empirical. The claim is no doubt still made that the sucking of snake-bites is a correct empirical procedure. It is in the perception of a man who thinks he knows a better empirical procedure that this becomes "magical." In short, *magic* appears to be a term used by some to refer to empirical procedures that we, ourselves, do not use or believe in.

When the definition of magic is applied to this empirical case, it explains aspects of primitive behavior and belief that were confusing when viewed by a nonparticipant in the system. The magical practices peculiar to any one primitive society may not be identical to those of others, yet they have a striking similarity in their ability to be explained in terms of personal magical power, empirical thought, and thus magical knowledge.

Benedict, for example, observed the strange behavior of the Kwakiutl in the face of the "shame" of death.[46] But this feeling of great shame (and consequent action) is not really so strange. It may be explained as the result of clear evidence by his death of the individual's lack of power. It might be expected that those related to him would feel shame. If individual success is measured in terms of success in action (power), this ultimate display of a lack of it is reason indeed for extreme shame.

Spiro, on the other hand, experienced some confusion in his analysis of witches. He noted that the Burmese belief in the existence of witches is "acquired by learning about them, rather than by experiences with them."[47] Yet he later observes the contrary, that such beliefs (he calls them "culturally structured fantasy systems") "are true, not only because they are transmitted with the authority of tradition, but because he [the individual] has personally experienced their truth."[48] Nevertheless, the obvious test of their "truth" is the test of experience. If they were taught but did not work, the magical thinker would provide another explanation. These particular beliefs are not "fantasy systems" forced on individuals by their culture or by authority, but *what is culturally determined is the framework in which certain types of beliefs may exist.* A small, simple, isolated society without a written language or an intelligentsia has neither the need nor the equipment to produce complex rationalized conceptual explanations. Empirical thought is the simplest type and there is no need nor ability to go beyond it. Thus, if a society fits the characteristics of primitive society, it should be expected that the system of knowledge present will be based on empirical thought and the notion of personal, individual power. Beliefs peculiar to individual primitive societies should be explainable in terms of this general theoretical conception.

[46] See Ruth Benedict, *Patterns of Culture* (Boston: Houghton Mifflin Company, 1934), p. 216.

[47] Spiro, *Burmese Supernaturalism*, p. 21.

[48] *Ibid.*, p. 72.

CHAPTER FIVE

SOCIAL STRUCTURE AND RELIGIOUS KNOWLEDGE

With DAVID WILLER

FROM MAGIC TO RELIGION

Magical and religious knowledge involve antithetical conceptions of power. Religious power is a rational conception which is not of this world; the search for power by man is regarded as futile. But in a magical system the conditions are different. Power is an attribute of men in this world and is not abstracted from it. Since magic relies exclusively on empirical thought connection while religious thought is primarily rational, disagreement about the nature of the world appears inevitable. The social conditions found where this conflict takes place will determine which of the two systems of knowledge will prevail.

Simply because magic presents a less complex type of knowledge, there must be conditions in which religious knowledge replaces it. Thus, when religious knowledge develops out of magical knowledge, there will be stages of that development in which the two types of knowledge are mixed. Such a mixed knowledge system would be characterized by the abstraction of *some* power from the world to another rationally conceived world in which power is also held. The world to which such power is abstracted may be regarded as too remote for man to reach. The gods (or power-holders) in this system might be as numerous as the concerns of man and not imperceptible, as in a pure religion, but merely somewhat remote from man's observation. They could even appear from time to time. Since all power is not abstracted from the world, man would not be powerless, and there would be a balance of powers between man and his gods. The idea of a nonmaterial, abstract soul would not be highly developed, and thus ideas of life after death might receive less emphasis and importance than in a fully developed religion. The emphasis in thought and action would still be in this world, and the purpose of worship of particular gods would be primarily in order to achieve worldly goals.[1]

This halfway point between magic and religion is represented in the classical Greek myths as well as in other systems of knowledge in Europe prior to the influence of Rome. The ideas found in the *Iliad* and *Odyssey*, for example, are consistent with the notion of a mixture of magic and religion. They are not rationalized with a number of gods representing various activities of concern to man in this world. The whole of the Greek pantheon (with Athena, goddess of wisdom; Aphrodite, goddess of love; Poseidon, god of the sea; Dionysus, god of wine; etc.) represents an abstraction of more magical spirits to Olympus which was originally simply a high mountain remote from man but which later was believed to be an abstract world. The world was not created by these gods but by powers who lived before them, and their power was more limited. Their power did not extend infinitely, but it was often necessary for them to appear in the world in order to produce the effects they desired. In this conception gods were regarded as observable, but were not necessarily observed. Their actions could not be accounted for by the cool rationalism of theology because irrationality was often attributed to them and consistent behavior thus not expected. Their motives often were hate, revenge, love, or desire, and in this sense they were anthropomorphic.

The stories of Hercules and Ulysses illustrate well the conception of man's relation to his gods in this type of knowledge system. Hercules' ancestry was half man and half god, and he was consequently endowed with power greater than that of ordinary men but less than that of the gods. Like the gods themselves, he was not thought to be particularly intelligent but was endowed with the qualities of a warrior hero. He was Zeus' son by a human and was disliked by Hera who tried to kill him but was unsuccessful

---

[1] Swanson has stated that there is an empirical connection between social organization and monotheism; but, in the absence of theoretical conceptualization his evidence is not convincing. Theoretically, there appears to be no reason why the god-concept, the rationally conceived power-holder, should consist of many individuals instead of one. The crucial requirement is that this be a rational concept. While Swanson made the mistake of identifying the existence of a "high god" with monotheism, his data were further rendered unconvincing by his failure to make a theoretical distinction between magic and religion. Primitive society has a less complex social organization, and no monotheism: there are no gods at all in purely magical knowledge systems. And more complex societies with greater social differentiation may well possess religious knowledge and a god-concept. On the other hand, complex social organization may be isomorphic with scientific knowledge, mysticism, and magic, as well as religion, depending upon how the social structure is divided. For Swanson's discussion see Guy E. Swanson, *The Birth of the Gods: The Origin of Primitive Beliefs* (Ann Arbor: The University of Michigan Press, 1960), pp. 65–66.

because of the power Hercules had derived from Zeus. He offended Zeus who required him to carry out twelve labors necessitating great power. In his last act as a mortal Hercules ascended to Olympus and there demanded that the gods grant him immortality and a place at their table, acquiring thereafter the status of a god.

Ulysses, on the other hand, was not endowed with superhuman powers, although he, like other higher status Greeks of the time, claimed descent from a god. A later figure than Hercules, Ulysses was attributed a certain degree of success because of his clever mind. It was through his trickery that both the Trojans and their gods were deceived by a hollow wooden horse into which his best men were to secret themselves and later climb out within Trojan walls to sack the city. However, this deed angered Poseidon, god of the sea and patron god of Troy, who caused Ulysses' ship to be blown around continuously from one place to another (where he was subjected to various hardships) for twenty years.

These myths describe the conceived nature of the Greek gods and thus present the structure of the system of knowledge. Acquaintance with the myths allowed the individual to understand the nature of the world and of gods and consequently to guide his actions. In order to have success in certain actions it was necessary to take into account the appropriate god or gods. The amount of power held by the individual would determine how he approached the gods, whether to coerce, supplicate, or make sacrifices. Sacrifice could either be in order to make contact or to bribe the appropriate god. On the other hand, the gods might be tricked or simply ignored.

Taken singly or together, the Greek gods were not omnipotent, omniscient, or omnipresent. They did not create the world, nor did they bestow immortality upon selected men. Men were thought to have life after death, but this was merely a residence for the souls which had departed from their bodies. These souls lived in Hades, an underworld which did not have the characteristics of the residence of the gods. (It was so dissimilar that it later became the basis for the Christian conception of Hell.) Life on earth was considered far better than residence in Hades.

Mixtures of magic and religion can take many forms. Diverse individual cases are conventionally described as pure religion, but it is also common for cases of religion to be classified as magic.

WEBER'S SOCIOLOGY OF RELIGION

Charisma, according to Weber, may be of two kinds, either that which is naturally inherent in objects or that which can be produced in them.[2]

---

[2] See Max Weber, *The Sociology of Religion*, trans. by E. Fischoff (Boston: Beacon Press, 1964), p. 2.

Both of these are found in magical systems where having charisma is equivalent to being full of magical power. But charisma of the second type is also found in religious systems. As a consequence of his relationship with the abstract power source, the religious leader may be a vessel of power and may be described as having charisma. Here the power is not an attribute of the individual himself, but it is derived from his relationship with his god who holds all power. The individual does not possess power but rather religious authority. Religious authority and magical power, although they may both be classified as charismatic, are quite different in meaning, regardless of occasional external similarities.

The relevant empirical distinctions are crucial here. Moses was able to deliver the Israelites from Egypt, not because he was a wizard or had special powers, but because of his unique relationship with his god. The Angel of Death was not a demon under the personal command of Moses but was an emissary of God sent against the Egyptians. The waters parted for the Jews, but they were parted by God, not Moses. Moses held charismatic authority rather than charismatic power—he was a prophet, not a magician.

Similarly, it was because of Jesus' relationship with God that the loaves and fishes were caused to multiply. It was God who healed the sick and brought the dead back to life rather than Jesus. Jesus held charismatic authority, not charismatic power, and he was thus a prophet instead of a magician.

The Catholic priest does not perform spells over the bread and wine to cause it to turn into flesh and blood. This is not a magical act, although it requires extraordinary power for its completion. The priest is not a wizard, nor does he claim to be. Such a claim would be to his mind the gravest possible sin. He exercises no personal power in such cases but instead authority, here routinized and related to his hierarchical position in the Church authority structure. He is not a magician.

This distinction is particularly clear from the point of view of any developed religion. To the practicing Christian, the assertion that Christ utilized magic in his actions is immediately rejected. Such an assertion is likely to be greeted with expressions of horror. This reaction is, of course, consistent with the idea structure of a religious system of knowledge. A Christian believes in the monopoly of power by his god, and the attribution of power to another amounts to a denial of the rational structure of his belief. (It is true, however, that in some Christian rationalizations the power-concept is split between God, Jesus, and the Holy Spirit; but in this case there is still a monopoly of power outside of the world since Jesus is not considered to be a human being.)

A prophet, according to Weber, is an individual who "by virtue of his mission proclaims a religious doctrine or divine commandment."[3] He may

---

[3] *Ibid.*, p. 46.

be a founder or a "renewer of religion."[4] But Weber claimed that this "in practice meant magic."[5] Prophets, as he pointed out, practice healing, counseling, and divination; but Weber confused the meaning of the action with its external manifestation. The crucial issue is not the superficial similarities of marvelous deeds, but rather the meaning to the individuals concerned which clearly divides the prophet from the magician. The magician has charismatic power which he holds himself. The prophet is an emissary of his power-concept (or god) and holds authority because of his relationship with his god. His extraordinary acts are associated with his mission, and both are a consequence of his relationship with the source of power, the god.

On the other hand, the founders of schools of philosophy such as Pythagoras and Confucius were not prophets in spite of the fact that they also taught the elements of a system of knowledge. They claimed no special relationship with an abstract power-concept, nor did they present their teachings as derived from that relationship. Mohammed, however, because he did make that claim, fits the definition of a prophet.

The distinguishing characteristic of a religious prophet cannot be charismatic authority alone, for charisma of this type is also held by priests. Priests and prophets, however, are quite different. Prophets create religion and are directly related to their gods, while priests continue religions and are related to their gods as a consequence of their position in an established religion.

In spite of occasional errors of this sort, Weber's sociology of religion is of central importance to the understanding of this type of knowledge system. A major weakness of contemporary studies of religion is that they ignore the theoretical issues which he concerned himself with: types of prophecy, the relation of religion to social structure, and the problem of theodicy. This is largely due to the empirical orientation of modern sociology. However, Weber did not offer an integrated theory of religion but a set of ideas which are empirically related under particular circumstances. In order to deal with these ideas and their empirical relations it will be necessary to compare them with the concepts of the theory of knowledge.

The term Weber used which most closely corresponds to "systems of knowledge" is "world religions." World religions are "systems of life regulation."[6] He includes in this category Confucianism, Hinduism, Buddhism, Christianity, Islam, and Judaism. The inclusion of Judaism makes it clear that size of membership is not the sole definitional criterion. World religions are systems of knowledge, but they refer apparently only to religious and mystical systems and exclude magical and scientific ones.

---

[4] *Ibid.*, p. 46.
[5] *Ibid.*, p. 47.
[6] Max Weber, *From Max Weber: Essays in Sociology*, trans. by H.H. Gerth and C.W. Mills (New York: Oxford University Press, 1958), p. 267.

Weber's use of the term "religion" is much broader and less specific than the meaning employed here. He refused to define religion at the outset of his work,[7] and did not get around to it later, although he used the term frequently. Since he did not formally define it, the meaning he employed was that in common use when he wrote and is not much different from that found in the United States today. Although Buddhism and Calvinism have different basic structures, both are included in the common notion of religion. As a result of this lack of formal definition, Weber frequently encountered difficulties when he attempted to make systematic statements, as when he attempted to analyze mysticism. In order to avoid such confusion, Weber's meaning will be ignored in the following discussion, even in the quoted material, and the meaning used will correspond to that of the theory of knowledge.[8]

Weber's terms, *zweckrational* and *wertrational,* are related to empirical and rational thinking, respectively. *Zweckrational* is a "rational orientation to a system of discrete individual ends"[9] while *wertrational* is defined as "involving a conscious belief in the absolute value of some ethical, aesthetic, religious, or other form of behavior, entirely for its own sake and independently of any prospects of external success."[10] Thus Weber meant two things by rationalism: "It means one thing if we think of the kind of rationalization the systematic thinker performs on the image of the world. . . . Rationalism means another thing if we think of the methodical attainment of a definitely given and practical end."[11]

Zweckrational (which is sometimes translated as "practical rationality") is empirical thought. *Wertrational* corresponds to theoretic knowledge and rational connection. Weber uses these terms in many contexts, and, because they correspond so closely to the terms of the theory of knowledge, connection of the theory to Weber's work is simplified. But Weber had no term for abstractive thought and therefore did not have a term to deal with the problem of connection between the theoretic and observational levels of thought. Such a concept seems necessary, however, to systematically handle mysticism and asceticism.

PROPHECY

Theology (or what Weber called "doctrine") consists of a "rational system of religious concepts."[12] Such a rational system is lacking in magic

[7] Weber, *Religion,* p. 1.

[8] The fact that this can effect the meaning of this material is recognized. The major effect will be a narrowing of meaning of the quoted material.

[9] Max Weber, *The Theory of Social and Economic Organization,* trans. by A.M. Henderson and T. Parsons (Glencoe: The Free Press, 1947), p. 115.

[10] *Ibid.,* p. 115.

[11] Weber, *Essays,* p. 293.

[12] Weber, *Religion,* p. 29.

and mysticism, while the rise of religion requires the development of a rational set of concepts, a theology. This is the task of ethical prophecy, one of two types of prophecy discussed by Weber. He pointed out that the ethical prophet is "an instrument for the proclamation of a god and his will, be this concrete command or an abstract norm. Preaching as one who has received a commission from god, he demands obedience as an ethical duty."[13] Ethical prophets "have not experienced themselves as vessels of the divine but rather as instruments of a god."[14] This type of prophecy is further distinguished by an "affinity to a special conception of God: the conception of a supra-mundane, personal, wrathful, forgiving, loving, demanding, punishing Lord of Creation."[15] The conception of a god which results from ethical prophecy is of one who created the world, the empirical reality surrounding man. This is a god in whom all power is concentrated while man is himself regarded as powerless; but man, having been created by the god, has ethical duties toward him. These ethical duties, which are a result of the conceived nature of god and man, define the nature of good and evil. The evil man is worldly and seeks power and pleasure in the empirical world. Evil, in other words, is closely connected with magical behavior. On the other hand, the man who accepts religion rejects worldly things. His actions are not governed by worldly ends but by the ethical system of his religion. The ethical system consists of theoretic norms which are connected by abstraction to specific empirical actions. As Weber pointed out, "To the prophet, both the life of man and the world, both social and cosmic events, have a certain systematic and coherent meaning."[16] But no single prophet presents a wholly rationalized conception of man, the world, and the power-concept. Prophecy is a major source of religious ideas, often *the* major source; but these ideas are not necessarily rationalized at the outset. Their place at the theoretic level, however, leaves them open to later rationalization and rational extension. As Weber noted, "A rationalization of metaphysical views and a specifically religious ethic are usually missing in the case of a cult without priests."[17]

It is clear, then, that prophecy alone, even if accepted by great masses of people, does not necessarily result in a fully developed religion. The conceptions put forward by prophets are "dominated, not by logical consistency, but by practical valuations."[18] The main contribution of prophets is religious terms or ideas at the theoretic level and their connection by abstraction to human behavior. Systemization of the ideas of prophets and their rational extension is the task of the theologians in the priesthood. "At first the priesthood itself was the most important carrier of intellectualism, par-

---

[13] *Ibid.*, p. 55.
[14] Weber, *Essays*, p. 285.
[15] *Ibid.*, p. 285.
[16] Weber, *Religion*, p. 59.
[17] *Ibid.*, p. 30.
[18] *Ibid.*, p. 59.

ticularly wherever sacred scriptures existed, which would make it necessary for the priesthood to become a literary guild engaged in interpreting the scriptures."[19] The product of this intellectualism is the increasingly complete rationalization of the theology.

The first division of mental labor in religion is between the prophet as creator of theoretic ideas and the theologian, a member of a priesthood, who relates these theoretic ideas as concepts in a rational system and rationally extends them. Soon, however, these two come into conflict. Prophecy is a necessary first stage in the development of religion; but, once concepts are rationalized, new prophecy may represent an irrational departure from established theology and ethics from the theologian's point of view. Furthermore, the priesthood has an interest in monopolizing the creation and interpretation of theological and ethical systems. As the priesthood develops, it becomes more able to maintain that monopoly. Consequently, prophecy is limited to the earliest stages of religious development. Later prophecies may be suppressed as heretical, meaning that they are not logically consistent with the developed systems, or may result in a separation from the organization controlled by the priesthood, forming a possible basis for the establishment of a new religious organization. Both of these outcomes may be expected where a religious organization has been established and authority monopolized by a priesthood.

From a scientific, mystical, or magical point of view, the prophet *creates* religious ideas. From his own point of view, he does not create them, but they are created by his god. The prophet merely communicates them. Nevertheless, it is the original communication of these ideas, which later become rational concepts in a theology, that is the distinguishing characteristic of a prophet. The priesthood consists of the theologians who rationalize religious concepts and the priests who apply them. Both, like the prophet, claim charismatic authority.

THEOLOGY

The basic characteristics of theologies, according to Weber, have been determined by the problem of theodicy and its solutions. Theodicy conventionally refers to the vindication of the justice of God in permitting the existence of evil. Weber states the problem of theodicy as follows:

> the more the development tends toward the conception of a transcendental unitary god who is universal, the more there arises the problem of how the extraordinary power of such a god may be reconciled with the imperfection of the world that he has created and rules over.[20]

Weber discussed four solutions to this problem offered by religions.

[19] *Ibid.*, p. 118.
[20] *Ibid.*, pp. 138–39.

One solution, the messianic, involves the belief in a just equalization in the future in which those favored by the god will be rewarded and given their rightful positions, while those not favored will be punished and put down. This may involve the 'return' of the god to earth or the movement of the souls of the favored to the god with life after death. Weber argued that this solution has never been carried to its logical conclusion in empirical cases.

Another solution is predestination, found in its purest forms in Calvinism and Islam. In the concept of predestination is the idea of a god so powerful and so abstract as to be unknowable by men; therefore men cannot understand his actions or the reasons for the existence of evil. Indeed, worldly imperfections may be interpreted as only apparent.[21]

An alternative solution is dualism in which the gods representing the good are opposed to autonomous powerful entities of darkness and evil. The evil of this world is therefore quite real and is a consequence of those evil powers. Dualism reached its purest form in Zoroasterism and Manicheism.[22]

On the other hand, Weber regarded the notion of the transmigration of souls as the most complete solution. Present ills arise as a result of previous sins which can be expiated by correct action in the world. If the present life is ethically meritorious, the rebirth of the soul can be in a higher, more advantaged, position or even in an abstract world. But life in that heaven can last only as long as warranted by accumulated merit. The purest case of this is found in Hinduism and is represented in the caste structure.[23]

Weber offered these descriptions of observed solutions to the problem of theodicy as he perceived it, but he did not offer a systematic explanation of the problem. The problem has as its basis a contradiction between the theology and the ethical system. The relationship between man and his god goes through a set of transformations as the god becomes more theoretic and powerful while man becomes correspondingly weak. When slightly removed from magic, the conception of god is theoretic but the aim of behavior still remains wholly practical. At this stage, the relation of the individual to his god is such that he asks, demands, supplicates, cajoles, or tricks the god to support his action in order to achieve success in some empirical goal. This stage was illustrated by the Greek myths.

Perceived from the point of view of the theory of knowledge, both empirically acting men and theoretic gods may be attributed power. From the viewpoint of men at this stage, the purpose of religious observance is to enlist that theoretic power for one's own goals, or at least to prevent action against them. Religious observance in this stage of development does not fit

---

[21] See *ibid.*, pp. 142–43.
[22] See *ibid.*, p. 144.
[23] See *ibid.*, p. 145.

the modern conception of worship, supplication, nor does it oblige man to follow any ethical rules.

The second stage is characterized by a complete abstraction of power. God is attributed all power, and man becomes powerless. God is thought to have established rules for man's behavior and demands than man follow them. If man follows these ethical demands he will be successful in his worldly goals; but if he attempts to go against the power relationship and ignores the god's demands, he will be unsuccessful in his goals. The god proclaimed by Moses fits this type.

The final stage of development is most removed from magic. God is conceived as all-powerful while man is powerless and under the god's ethical control; but, although the god has established rules for man's behavior, success in worldly actions does not depend upon whether they are followed. Nevertheless, if man does follow the rules he may be rewarded in some rationally conceived world, as in the Christian Heaven, or punished in an unpleasant rationally conceived world, as in Hell. This conception is found in its pure form in some of the Christian sects.

Only in its final stages is the power-concept conceived as omnipotent, and thus only these stages represent pure religion. The first stage is intermediate between magic and religion; of the latter two religious stages, the final stage is more rationalized in that rewards and punishments are also abstracted from the world. Since rewards and punishments are no longer observable, there is no evidence in the empirical world which will contradict the god's power.

As the god becomes more powerful, man becomes less so, and the ethical system is developed along with the demand of obedience to the power-concept. Theologically the result of the conception of a unitary, all-powerful god is predestination. If the god has these qualities, the conception of predestination follows as a necessary consequence if the theological system is completely rationalized. If the god alone holds power, then all events are determined by him; all those which have occurred, are presently occurring, and will occur are a result of his will. Thus the god also must be all-knowing since he knows what the future will bring and indeed has already determined it. Man lives in the finite present of his existence whereas the power-concept must be simultaneously present throughout eternity. He exists at all times and all places equally.

That the idea of predestination is a logically necessary consequence of the rationalization of a religious system does not mean that it always appears. But, when it is present, it means that man's free will is entirely eliminated. If all is predetermined, then no freedom of choice is possible. From a theological viewpoint the idea of predestination has much to recommend it. In addition to being a consistent elaboration of the idea of an omnipotent god, it explains man's actions in the world. Religion, because it conceives of man as powerless, raises the question of how he can act in this world if devoid of power. But if a power-concept is the cause of all action, then this is sufficient to explain activity in the world.

Nevertheless, the idea of predestination and the theological conception of an all-powerful god coupled with an ethical system are contradictory. If man has an ethical responsibility to god, he must have the power to act with or against god's wishes, but this is impossible if god has all the power. It implies that all is not predetermined by god and that man has free will. Thus the existence of two separate types of thinking in a religious system of knowledge, the rationality of the theology and the abstraction of the ethic, leads to an inherent contradiction. The problem which Weber posed was not primarily the problem of theodicy, the vindication of god's justice in light of the existence of evil, but was a problem of contradiction between the simultaneous existence of ethic and theology in religion. The abstractive ethical component of religion assumes that man can act and ties ideals to action at the observational level. But the rational theological component of religion, in that it is completely severed from ties with the observational level, concludes that man cannot act. This contradiction is inherent in pure religion.

That the problem is inherent does not mean that it will be faced. St. Thomas Aquinas, for example, discusses the question of man's responsibility for his actions and God's infinite power quite separately. He attributes all power to God in a portion of his work quite separate from that in which he discusses man's free will to choose between good and evil. Thus even this great rationalist chose not to confront the problem. Calvin, on the other hand, argued consistently for the notion of predestination and concluded that man could not have free will. In his conception man was saved or damned from birth. To those who objected to the concept of election, Calvin replied that man is too insignificant to understand God's justice. But, as Weber pointed out, Calvin's concept of election in practice actually increased the effectiveness of his ethical system in spite of logically negating it.

Predestination is not a solution to the problem of theodicy but part of the contradiction. The contradiction is basic and, although it can be obscured, it cannot be solved. Weber's discussion of predestination involves Calvin's idea that the contrast between man and God is so great that man cannot really understand God at all. If man lacks the power of understanding, the theological-ethical contradiction is only apparent and is merely a consequence of man's complete ignorance. Man is not here attributed free will but is elected to salvation or damnation by God from the beginning of time. If this does not appeal to one's notion of justice, that in itself merely demonstrates the powerlessness to properly understand God. If the ethic is emphasized, the elect necessarily follow God's demands *because* they lack free will. Emphasis on the theology leads to fatalism. Calvin may have solved the problem of theodicy, but he did not eliminate the contradiction behind it.

The messianic view does not solve the abstractive-rational contradiction but does not ever reach it because the logical implications of the power-concept are not fully rationalized. Man is granted the power of decision, and the power-concept does not become all-powerful. Thus the conception of the god's power is considerably reduced from that of a fully rationalized religion. Man has free will and may choose not to follow god's laws. Resulting rewards or punishments may be either observable or theoretic.

In order to remain a pure religion, the theology must be rationalized and an ethic must be present. Predestination solves the problem of theodicy by ignoring the implications of the ethic, and the messianic view solves it by ignoring the implications of the theology, but neither of them is able to resolve the basic contradiction between ethic and theology.

The messianic conception amounts to a triumph of the ethical system over the theology. When the emphasis is upon abstract rewards and punishments, the main appeal of this conception is to those who are powerless in this world and wish to improve their condition in another. This includes especially the lower classes. When the emphasis is on immediate rewards and punishments in the present world, the appeal is to higher class groups. When the emphasis is on rewards and punishments in the empirical world at some future time, the appeal is to marginal ethnic groups such as the Jews.

Dualism likewise does not solve the contradiction between ethic and theology. Here either all power is monopolized by two rationally opposed entities and man is a powerless puppet whose actions are determined by the pull of one or the other and therefore cannot follow ethical demands, or man shares power with the two entities. Only the former case is pure religion. The latter case is mixed with magic and spells are used, as in New England Puritanism, to ward off evil spirits. In religious dualism the existence of evil in the world is explained by dividing the theoretic power-concept in two, half good and half evil. They may be equally balanced powers or, as in Christianity, the evil power may be subordinate to the good in the hope of gaining the advantages of dualism as a solution to the problem of theodicy without having to give up the idea of a single omnipotent god.

Dualism may explain the existence of evil in the world; however, it does not solve the contradiction of rationalism and abstraction but merely obscures it. Individual violations of the ethical rules can be explained by reference to the evil power; suffering by those who do obey the rules is similarly explained. The problem of theodicy is solved but not the contradiction in thought behind it.

Theologians must encounter the inherent contradiction in religion, but they may ignore it or adopt one of the "solutions" to the problem of theodicy. The developments of the Christian religion have resorted to all of these actions, sometimes separately and sometimes in combination (although they are not all logically compatible). Attempts to rationalize the basic contradiction of religion have kept generations of theologians busy.

THE KARMA DOCTRINE

The Hindu idea of karma, the transmigration of souls, is, according to Weber, the "most complete formal solution to the problem of theodicy."[24] He described this system in the following way:

> Guilt and merit within this world are unfailingly compensated by fate in the successive lives of the soul, which may be reincarnated innumerable times in animal, human, or even divine forms. . . . The finiteness of earthly life is the consequence of the finiteness of good or evil deeds in the previous life of a particular soul. What may appear from the viewpoint of a theory of compensation as unjust suffering in the terrestrial life of a person should be regarded as atonement for sin in a previous existence. Each individual forges his own destiny exclusively, in the strictest sense of the word.[25]

He concluded:

> The mechanism of retribution is, therefore, a consistent deduction from the super-divine character of the eternal order of the world, in contrast to the notion of a god who is set over the world, rules it personally, and imposes predestination upon it.[26]

Weber was correct in his conclusion that the karma doctrine does not have the same logical difficulties as the religious systems just discussed. In that sense it may be more logically satisfactory, but it is not a solution to the problem of theodicy. According to Weber, the problem of theodicy arises from the contrast between the all-powerful god and the imperfect world. But the karma system works without the intervention of a power-concept at all. God has no role in this deterministic system; therefore, there is no problem of theodicy in the karma system because no all-powerful god is needed or postulated. The karma system is, in fact, not a religious system at all but a magical one in which the individual determines his own destiny by his actions and in which the world is perceived to have a deterministic

[24] *Ibid.*, p. 145.
[25] *Ibid.*, p. 145.
[26] *Ibid.*, p. 146.

order, an idea which is necessary in a magical system in order to utilize empirical thinking and observation of order as a basis for action. The idea of the soul surviving the body (not because some power-concept *saved* it) is also a characteristic of magical knowledge systems.

In addition to the Indian conception of the soul, there are three basic elements of the karma system of knowledge: karma, the idea of rebirth; dharma, the idea of proper action; and varna or caste, the idea of status grouping. These ideas are related. All living beings, including man, have souls which do not cease to exist at death but are thought to be passed on to another body. The souls of men can pass into other types of creatures and vice versa. There are proper actions for all living beings according to their positions in life, and the caste into which men are born determines their action or dharma. All beings are arranged in a rank order from lowest to highest with the caste positions of men included in the structure. Those beings whose actions fit their dharma build up during their lives a certain amount of spiritual power. The amount of spiritual power thus accumulated determines whether the soul will be reborn at a higher rank. Those souls who do not follow their dharma will lose power, and consequent rebirth will be at a lower rank. Action in the present life is viewed as being completely free, and the individual may or may not follow his dharma as he chooses. The individual uses his own actions to accumulate power to advance his position in the next life; and, if he follows his dharma properly it is inevitable that he will be born in a higher position in his next life. This necessity, however, results from the natural order of the world, and no god intercedes in the process.

Because power is not abstracted from the world, because man may determine his position by his own actions, the karma system is not, by definition, a religion and thus cannot have a theodicy problem. Instead, as in a magical system, the karma system is inherently isomorphic with observations because it is based on empirical thinking. Present ills are a result of the free action of individuals when their souls existed in some previous life. Proper action may not lead to reward in the present life, but it does lead to the accumulation of power for higher rebirth. Virtue and reward are connected, but this connection is not simply in the present life but in the succession of lives of the individual. In fact, since this is a magical system, it may be a mistake to refer to a succession of lives, but one should instead note the life giving characteristic of souls which do not stop living between bodies but first give life to one body and then to another. It is only bodies which die for the empirical reason that only bodies are observed to die.

The magic of the karma system is somewhat different from that found in a less complex society. The karma doctrine explains the widespread disparity of wealth which is possible in a population much larger than that found in primitive society. It offers the possibility of mobility through rebirth when mobility is not possible considering the discrepancy between the rich and the poor. Conformity to the dharma both allows the individual hope for a better existence and tends to maintain the rigid social structure. Although the individual is responsible for his actions and may accumulate power, the karma system differs from the typical magical system in the sense that relative power is not gained through competition with others but is fixed according to whether the individual has followed a fixed set of actions corresponding to his fixed present position. Thus the karma system has a rigidity which is not present in the magical systems of primitive society. The karma system, in fact, tends to maintain the social structure as it is through pressure to conformity. The question remains, therefore, whether it is in the interest of some status group to promote a system whose magical character fits the empirical thinking of the poorer groups but which presents, in fact, a more logical character and a more rigid structure than is typically found in primitive society.

Although the lower castes in India fit closely the characteristics of primitive society in which magical knowledge is expected to exist, and although their actions are viewed as leading to individual power, the result of these actions, the reward of power itself is not observable. This leads to the possibility that, although these lower castes have no rational ideas of their own, there may be some caste which does utilize rational thought. The highest caste, the Brahman caste, does in fact have an interest in maintaining the social structure as it is (since they are in the most advantaged position) and does show evidence of possessing some elements of rational thinking. Rationalistic concepts, such as the positional number system with the concept of a zero and negative numbers, have developed in India. The reference in the number system to negative numbers as "debts" indicates the possibility that there had developed at least the beginnings of a rational system of cost accounting. The Brahman caste had the wealth and consequently the time to develop rational thinking, and therefore these and other evidences of rational thinking are not surprising.

It is also evident, however, that rational thought did not attain the same level of development in India that it did in the religious, mathematical, and scientific knowledge of Europe. But, considering the primitiye conditions which have prevailed throughout India's history and the consequent inability of rational thought to have much effect, this is not difficult to explain. The caste structure itself tended to maintain magical thinking for the lower castes and to keep them isolated from the upper castes and thus from the possibility of rational thinking. Difference of social conditions and isolation from rational thinking did not provide the conditions for the development of religion in India as a predominant system of knowledge. The Brahman castes developed and promoted the karma system in India which acts as a magical system for the lower castes and preserves and allows rationality in the upper castes, but they did not develop religion in spite of the seeming rationality of parts of the karma system. In order to *be* a religious system, it would have to operate as such.

RELIGIOUS SYSTEMS AND SOCIAL STRUCTURE

The nature of religion, according to Weber, is not simply a function of the social structure or the group within it which accepts it, and it is not determined by ideological or material interests of that group.

> However incisive the social influences, economically and politically determined, may have been upon a religious ethic in a particular case, it receives its stamp primarily from religious sources.[27]

Here Weber's position agrees with that of Troeltsch which may be summarized as follows:

> Christianity was not the product of a class struggle of any kind. . . . [But it was addressed] primarily to the oppressed. . . . The central problem is always purely religious.[28] . . . [Social issues] were lost sight of in the supreme question of eternal salvation and the appropriation of a spiritual inheritance. . . . the values of redemption were still purely inward, ethical, and spiritual.[29] . . . [The] appeal of Christianity to the lower classes had nothing to do with a "class" movement. . . . Poverty and simplicity are the foundation of truth.[30]

Troeltsch believed that Christianity is not a religion of social reform, a religion for the poor, but appeals to the poor primarily because one can find an "honest and good heart" more readily among the poor.[31]

Weber's viewpoint also agreed to some extent with Nietzsche's. He agreed that the evolution of suffering has radically changed with the development of religion, as Nietzsche claimed, and that the acceptance of a developed religion is a class phenomenon. In other words, Weber agreed with Nietzsche to the extent that Nietzsche agreed with Troeltsch.

Weber's position is in many ways unfortunate. He agreed that acceptance of developed religion is class related, but he argued that the basic content of theology is "religiously" caused. For an acknowledged religious man such as Troeltsch this position is understandable—theology is based in

[27] Weber, *Essays*, p. 270.

[28] Ernst Troeltsch, *The Social Teaching of the Christian Churches*, Vol. I, trans. by Olive Wyon (New York: The Macmillan Company, 1931), p. 39.

[29] *Ibid.*, p. 40.

[30] *Ibid.*, p. 46.

[31] *Ibid.*, p. 59.

the reality of religion. One does not expect Troeltsch to admit a social basis for religion, but it is somewhat different for a professed social scientist to take an identical position.

From the point of view of a religious system of knowledge, the content of religion is determined by the abstract power and is not created by man at all; but from a scientific point of view, religion is a product of society and is created by man. Gods are concepts of men, not the active forces some men have believed them to be. There is no empirical referent for gods, and isomorphism with empirical phenomena is necessary for acceptance of concepts in a scientific system of knowledge. Here there is no consistent middle road. When a rational explanation may be abstractively connected with empirical events, it is acceptable scientific knowledge; but a rational explanation which may not be so connected must be rejected in favor of any other explanation which may, no matter how poor the connection. From a religious point of view, scientific theories which contradict theology are false. From a scientific point of view, theologies which contradict scientific theories must be rejected for lack of isomorphism. Everyone may choose his own point of view (or accepts his point of view because of his position in his society); but this work is intended to be a scientific one, and thus the social explanation for the existence of religion is the one which is here adopted.

It is probable that Weber was not taking a mixed or irrational position. He was not devout, and had no faith of his own to explain. His position, instead, seems to have been that different social institutions often develop according to their own internal logic or causes and not simply as a consequence of external causes. This type of explanation might fit a magical system of knowledge in which things are attributed volition or a religious one in which religion is part of the true nature of things, but it is a dubious scientific explanation.

To argue that religion is not part of the nature of things but represents instead one of a number of possible systems of knowledge and has a basis in culture, is to argue an irreligious position. It has been a tradition in the United States that religious beliefs should be tolerated, and the majority of students of religion have either had a vested interest in religion (having a religious background of their own) or have been empiricist thinkers whose work never encounters ideas at the theoretic level. Thus there has been little effort to produce scientific studies of religion, although many sociologists would argue that their purely empirical work is scientific. Such thinkers as Marx and Engels and Nietzsche, however, have attempted to make theoretic statements about religion and have contributed to our scientific understanding of it in spite of the fact that their work is often interpreted as an attack upon religion.

The crucial area of disagreement between Nietzsche and Marx and

Engels, on the one hand, and Weber, on the other, is in the determination of the form and content of theological and ethical systems. Only Weber argued in favor of wholly religious causes, but they all agreed that the acceptance of religion is effected by social position. It is not acceptance but determination which is questioned.

Nietzsche preferred magic to religion: "What is good? Everything that heightens the feeling of power in man, the will to power, power itself. What is bad? Everything that is born of weakness."[32] Nietzsche (who did not have the concern for objectivity of the modern sociologist) felt no need to maintain "value neutrality." He did not simply outline a theory but argued strongly for a position. And, with the exception for his preference for mysticism over religion, he argued consistently for magical knowledge. He limited his discussion of religion to Christianity, but his analysis may be applied to any religion.

Taking a magical position, Nietzsche affirmed the world and the accumulation of power and rejected opposed religious valuations: "Life itself is to my mind the instinct for growth, for durability, for an accumulation of forces, for *power*; where the will to power is lacking there is decline."[33] Evidence of this decline is that religion favors

> all that is weak and base, with all failures; it has made an ideal of whatever *contradicts* the instinct of the strong life to preserve itself.[34] . . . Pity is the *practice* of nihilism. . . . It multiplies misery and conserves all that is miserable.[35] . . . The pure spirit is the pure lie. . . . Whoever has theologians' blood in his veins, sees all things in a distorted and dishonest perspective to begin with.[36] . . . Wherever the theologians' instinct extends, *value judgments* have been stood on their heads and the concepts of "true" and "false" are of necessity reversed: whatever is most harmful to life is called "true"; whatever elevates it, enhances, affirms, justifies it, and makes it triumphant is called "false."[37]

Nietzsche's critique of religion is what is expected of an individual with a magical viewpoint if viewed in terms of the theory of knowledge. He was correct in seeing the abstraction of power from the world as a characteristic of developed religion. His discussion of pure idealism corresponds to the discussion here of religious rationalism. Magical and religious ideas *are* in contradiction in terms of the location of power and in terms of the type of thought connection made. Nietzsche objected to the character of religious

---

[32] Friedrich Nietzsche, *The Portable Nietzsche*, selected and trans. by Walter Kaufmann (New York: The Viking Press, 1954), p. 570.

[33] *Ibid.*, p. 572.

[34] *Ibid.*, p. 571.

[35] *Ibid.*, p. 573.

[36] *Ibid.*, p. 575.

[37] *Ibid.*, p. 576.

thought which he criticized as pure idealism, separated from reality; and the placement of power was considered even more important. Because power is abstracted in religion, religious ideas stand in opposition to the search for power in life, the instinct for a strong life. From a magical viewpoint, value judgments are stood on their heads, truth and falsity are reversed.

But what is the source of religious ideas? Nietzsche asserted that the "preponderance of feelings of displeasure over feelings of pleasure is the cause of. . . religion."[38]. . . "Those who suffer must be maintained by a hope that can never be contradicted by any reality or be disposed of by any fulfillment—a hope of the beyond."[39] He added that "the instinct of *ressentiment*, which had here become genius, had to invent *another* world."[40] Nietzsche found the source of ressentiment primarily in the "lowest classes" and, in particular, in the "underworld of the ancient world."[41] He observed:

> The slaves' revolt in morals begins with this, that *ressentiment* itself becomes creative and gives birth to values: the *ressentiment* of those who are denied the real reaction, that of the deed, and who compensate with an imaginary revenge. Whereas all noble morality grows out of a triumphant affirmation of oneself, slave morality immediately says No to what comes from outside, to what is different, to what is not oneself: and *this* No is its creative deed. This reversal of the value-positing glance—this *necessary* direction outward instead of back to oneself—is the nature of *ressentiment*: to come into being, slave morality requires an outside world, a counterworld; physiologically speaking, it requires external stimuli in order to react at all: its action is at bottom always a reaction.[42]

For Nietzsche the basic question is, "Why suffer?" Religion offers an explanation which is accepted by the lower classes and all others for whom the pain found in life outweighs the pleasure. But, once established, religion glorifies suffering and, in doing so, continues the conditions needed for its existence. The crucial element, Nietzsche pointed out, is the distribution of suffering. The distribution of suffering is at least partially dependent upon the stratification of society. Weber was correct in pointing out that Nietzsche's theory implied a class determination of religion.

In order to see the theoretic import of Nietzsche's work, much that remains implicit in it must be made explicit. He argued that before the "slave revolt in morals," a more desirable condition existed. But social conditions changed, and with this change came necessarily a change in the type of thought.

With the expansion of the Roman Empire the conditions of existence of the least advantaged segments of society were comparatively worsened.

[38] *Ibid.*, p. 582.
[39] *Ibid.*, p. 591.
[40] *Ibid.*, p. 593.
[41] *Ibid.*, p. 589.
[42] *Ibid.*, p. 451.

Under a rationalized administration they were rendered powerless. Mental and manual labor became widely separated; and, in the presence of written language, theoretic thought developed separately from empirical thought. Nietzsche pointed out that it was under these conditions that Christianity arose in the West.

His argument, in terms of the theory of knowledge, was that, since they were now powerless, magical knowledge no longer fit the conditions of existence of these disadvantaged groups. Religion, because it rejected the world and abstracted all power from the world, fit better the conditions of their existence. A feeling of *ressentiment* toward those who made them power-less arose from the socially powerless and found its expression in religious doctrine. Fitting their conditions of existence was the requirement that being ascetic was good while worldliness was evil.

In contrast to religion, magic offered nothing to these classes. In magic, power is the good while powerlessness is the bad, but these classes were all powerless. Clearly there was no basis for hope in their present exist-ence, and Nietzsche's analysis implies that religious ideas would be selected from those available because they both offered hope and were compatible with the conditions of existence. This, of course, is only part of the expla-nation.

Marx viewed religion as "the *opium* of the people."[43] As Weber indi-cated, Marx and Engels considered religion to be a reflection of social con-ditions. If religion is an opium and inhibits other behaviors, particularly political ones, it may be asked how it can at the same time reflect the social conditions of the disadvantaged. From Marx's view, religion is "*a reversed world-consciousness* . . . the *reflexion* of [man] himself."[44] . . . "The religious world is but the reflex of the real world."[45] This reversal is expressed in con-tradictions between earthly conditions and religious concepts—"between mind and matter, man and nature, soul and body."[46] He could well have included heaven and earth, predestination and free will, and god and man.

In the most simple state of society men have not separated ideas from material objects and empirical happenings; all thinking is empirical. Here, where social relations are simple, man confronts nature, and his struggle for existence is primarily a struggle with nature. This is the basis of the forma-tion of his consciousness, and, instead of religion, a "consciousness of nature"[47] results which seems essentially equivalent to what is here termed magic. Development from the primitive state necessarily means the development of the division of labor:

[43] Karl Marx and Friedrich Engels, *On Religion* (New York: Schocken Books, 1964), p. 42.

[44] *Ibid.*, p. 41.

[45] *Ibid.*, p. 135.

[46] *Ibid.*, p. 188.

[47] *Ibid.*, p. 75.

> The division of labour becomes real division only from the instant when the division of material and spiritual labour takes place. From this instant con- sciousness *can* really fancy that it is something else than consciousness of existing practice, that it *really* imagines something without imagining anything real; from this instant consciousness is able to emancipate itself from the world and to go on to the forming of 'pure' theory, theology, philosophy, morals, etc.[48]

The division of spiritual or mental from manual labor means the first development of theoretic ideas, concepts and rational thought. Here, as Marx and Engels point out, ideas are no longer merely labels for empirical objects and existing practice. Since the development of theoretic ideas is dependent upon this division of mental and manual labor, it is a necessary condition for the development of theology and thus of religion. Religion cannot develop in primitive society in which ideas are tied only to objects and existing practice. The description of primitive consciousness given by Marx and Engels fits the conception of primitive thinking connected with magical knowledge. The development of theology thus requires a changed basis of thinking (from empirical to rational) which goes along with a fun- damental change in social structure, the introduction of separate mental labor.

Before mental and manual labor are separated, they are not in con- tradiction. All men are both mental and manual laborers, and thought and existence are necessarily connected. This conclusion not only explains primitive empiricism but also the lack of contradiction between primitive ideas and their observable conditions of existence. Once the two types of labor are separated, they "can and must enter into contradiction with one another, because the *division of labor* implies the possibility, nay, the reality, that spiritual and material activity—enjoyment and work, production and consumption fall to different individuals."[49] Marx and Engels see in this contradiction the source of religion.

Religions are not founded by the most disadvantaged classes. They cannot be founded by the disadvantaged, for the disadvantaged are manual laborers who are separated from the means of mental production and thus from theoretic thought. As in the development of working class movements, outside ideologists are needed. This results, according to Marx, in "the first form of ideologists (priests)."[50] Engels observed in addition that "Religions are founded by people who feel a need for religion themselves and have a feeling for the religious needs of the masses."[51] In fact, he argued that the "history of early Christianity has notable points of resemblance with the

[48] *Ibid.*, p. 76.
[49] *Ibid.*, pp. 76–77.
[50] *Ibid.*, p. 76.
[51] *Ibid.*, p. 197.

modern working class movement."[52] After all, both are based on theoretic thought and recruit from analogous class positions.

At the beginning, according to Marx and Engels, man's thought reflects the forces of nature; but soon, with increasing social complexity and intensity of social interaction, thought comes to reflect social forces. Man is dominated by alien social and economic forces which are powers outside himself and creates religion as a reflection of that domination.[53] As long as social life dominates man instead of man dominating social life, the "actual basis of the reflective activity that gives rise to religion therefore continues to exist, and with it the religious reflection itself."[54] Under these conditions, religion should have some appeal to all groups, not just the disadvantaged.

The appeal of religious knowledge is also viewed as a result of the division of labor. With it stratification develops, and with stratification differential satisfaction. In the disadvantaged stratum distress is concentrated. "*Religious* distress is at the same time the *expression* of real distress and the *protest* against real distress."[55] During the development of the Empire, Roman administration and military power put an end to independent states, and, through the pressure of taxation, plunged most classes into debt.

> Any resistance of isolated small tribes or towns to the gigantic Roman world power was hopeless. Where was the way out, salvation, for the enslaved, oppressed and impoverished, a way out common to all these groups of people whose interests were mutually alien or even opposed? And yet it had to be found if a great revolutionary movement was to embrace them all.[56]

With the growth of Christianity, asceticism became a valued way of life isomorphic to the conditions of life of the lower strata.[57] "To all complaints about the wickedness of the times ... Christian consciousness of sin answered."[58]

Although religion offers salvation from the social conditions of distressed and oppressed groups, it does not offer relief through social revolution but in an abstract world after death. Engels argued that the Christian movement was based on the same motives as later socialist movements, but Marx pointed out that its ultimate effect was conservative rather than radical:

> The social principles of Christianity justified the slavery of Antiquity, glorified

---

[52] *Ibid.*, p. 316.
[53] See *ibid.*, p. 148.
[54] *Ibid.*, p. 148.
[55] *Ibid.*, p. 42.
[56] *Ibid.*, p. 335.
[57] See *ibid.*, p. 336.
[58] *Ibid.*, p. 203.

the serfdom of the Middle Ages and equally know, when necessary, how to defend the oppression of the proletariat, although they make a pitiful face over it.[59]

Marx reasoned: "it teaches, as religion must: Submit to authority for *all authority* is ordained by God."[60]

Finally, Engels saw the Protestant Reformation as also based on economic changes, particularly the development of capitalism. First Lutheran, then more importantly Calvinist, doctrine fit the developing bourgeois class. "His [Calvin's] predestination doctrine was the religious expression of the fact that in the commercial world of competition success or failure does not depend upon a man's activity or cleverness, but upon circumstances uncontrollable by him."[61]

Obviously Marx and Engels did not have a systematic theory of religion. In fact, much of what they said about religion is to be found in offhand comments in works whose main concern was quite different. Still, these ideas are valuable and deserve consideration in the theory of religious knowledge.

The importance of the division of mental from manual labor was pointed out in an earlier chapter in relation to magical knowledge. It was indicated that under the social conditions of primitive society magic would be all-pervasive. In preliterate societies with little division of labor, thought and practice are not separated, and the type of thinking is empirical. Since power thus cannot be abstracted, this situation is characterized by magical knowledge. When a society becomes more complex, its division of labor increases; this may happen in a number of ways, the most important to the theory of knowledge being the separation of mental from manual labor without which thought cannot be separated from immediate practice. The separation of thought from immediate practice is a necessary, but not sufficient, condition for the rise of theoretic thought.

The development of theoretic thought requires the use of symbols not tied to empirical objects. In man's history one such symbol system has been particularly important, the phonetically written word system. In order for such a symbol system to develop, the separation of mental labor must have occurred.

The written phonetic word, in contrast to drawn pictographic language, is not necessarily connected to empirical objects. The connection of word to word is potentially a rational connection. This is not the case with pictographs which are drawn specifically to represent objects or acts and cannot be separated from empirical thinking. The phonetically written word

---

[59] *Ibid.*, p. 83.
[60] *Ibid.*, p. 37.
[61] *Ibid.*, p. 301.

is not necessarily a theoretic concept, but it is not necessarily an empirical category either. When used by those who practice mental labor only, it can be separated from the empirical and may develop meaning from its association with other words. When that occurs, the use is theoretic. On the other hand, as in the case of Locke and the British Empiricists, the meaning may be deliberately limited to the empirical with resultant elimination of theoretic connection. The British Empiricists, however, were empirical thinkers through rejection of rational thinking in contrast to the primitives. Their choice of empirical thinking was made through a conscious reaction to religion.

The existence of rational thinking is thus not necessitated by the presence of a written system of symbols. A contrast may be made between the Indian and Greek schools of philosophy. Thinkers who did not concern themselves with the plight of the relatively powerless manual laborer produced philosophy, while those who were involved with the problems of the less fortunate classes became involved in the development of religion. The development of religion involves the synthesis of theoretic thought with the conditions of existence of powerless manual laborers who are themselves separated from the means of mental production. The uneducated, powerless, manual laboring classes are unable to develop religion, although their social conditions are no longer compatible with magical knowledge. Religion is first developed by men whose position in the social structure is marginal: they are powerless like the manual laborer, but they have been trained in mental skills. It is, of course, only a rare individual who is found in such circumstances; but these social conditions are compatible with the development of religion. The prophet, like Jesus Christ, is a marginal man, a powerless mental laborer.

STRATIFICATION AND RELIGION

When mental and manual labor is divided, power is no longer shared by all, as it was in primitive society. In Table 3 the circles and boxes represent social positions, and the lines represent communications. Figure 1 represents a totally related group in which there is communication between all individuals in all positions, the characteristic structure of a small, primitive society. Some individuals may have more power and influence than others, but the structure does not determine their ascendancy. Whatever stratification occurs in this type of structure is entirely dependent upon the special *powers* of individuals. Otherwise power is shared. Because of the great number of lines of communication in this structure, it is highly inefficient for complex tasks which require coordination. Therefore, even some of the most primitive societies take on the structure of Figure 2 for efficiency of coordination,

TABLE 3. SOCIAL STRATIFICATION AND COMMUNICATION LINES

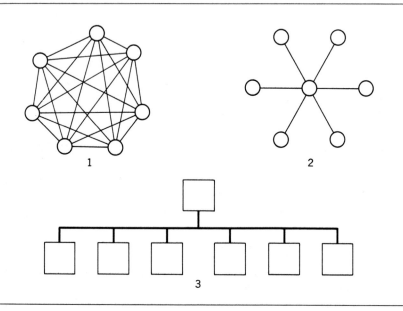

particularly for war. If they took on this form permanently and extended it to economic behavior, they would have, in effect, moved away from the pure primitive type.

Figure 2 represents a centrality group. There is a central position and a group of peripheral ones, and the number of relationships or communications between individuals is much less, 6 instead of the 15 in Figure 1. A group of this structure can be more easily coordinated because of the efficiency gained through the limited communication requirements. Its connectivity pattern is like that of Figure 3, which is an organization chart. Most task organizations in most nonprimitive societies take the form represented in Figure 2, and the need for such a structure varies with group size. The number of relationships (R) is a function of N, the number of people. For the structure represented in Figure 1, the number of relationships is determined by the equation, $R = N\dfrac{N-1}{2}$. For the structure found in Figure 2, the equation is $R = N - 1$. If time needed for communication is proportional to the number of relationships, then whenever there is a need for efficiency, the structure in Figure 2 will develop if the group is to survive. Only primitive social groups that manage to remain isolated from other groups characteristically maintain the structure of Figure 1. When isolation does not prevail, either the structure changes or the group does not survive.

Figure 2 represents the first division of labor, and Figure 3 represents the first division of mental from manual labor. The individuals in Figure 2 who are in the peripheral positions possess less power than the one in the center, whereas the structural difference in Figure 3 is based on a position of authority at the top. If power becomes concentrated in the center of the structure in Figure 2, the efficiency gained through the use of this structure (rather than Figure 1) may be utilized to provide extra time for the central figure while those at the edges provide the manual labor for his support. This freedom from manual labor, allows the central individual the time to develop mental connections, and provides the initial conditions needed for the development of theoretic thought. The development of theoretic thought provides the preconditions for the development of religious knowledge and authority. Figure 3 therefore is the structure typical of religious systems in which the central position is not a position of power, but one built into the structure. It is not a position which is an empirical position gained by the individual with most power, but is a rationally fixed structural position occupied by individuals who gain authority by that occupation.

The final condition for the development of religion is the abstraction of power to the theoretic level, an abstraction which is isomorphic with the idea of concentration of power in central positions. The result is theology, and the result of complete abstraction of power from the social structure is an authoritarian basis of stratification. The abstraction of power to a theoretic position is isomorphic to the increasing powerlessness of individuals in peripheral positions in the social structure. They are powerless in a way in which individuals in more primitive societies are not, and the central position becomes more separated and thus more fixed. When those in peripheral positions are powerless and the basis of stratification is in the central position itself rather than in a central individual, all individuals in the structure are powerless, and magical knowledge is no longer meaningful.

The comments of Marx and Engels and of Nietzsche concerning the rise of religion in the Roman Empire may be explained by analyzing its structure of centrality—the largest of its type ever to have existed until that time. Its efficient, administrative structure rendered more people powerless than ever before. Because of the prior division of mental from manual labor, theoretic thought had already developed. In the Roman Empire, therefore, both the social conditions isomorphic to religion and the abstraction of power from the world and the mental tools by which to develop a rational system were present. The power-authority structure was precisely that necessary for the development of religion.

The analysis of the relations between knowledge systems and social structure and stratification agrees, on the whole, with many points made by Marx and Engels, and it may be used to explain some of their more disconnected views. Religious distress is an expression of social distress in the sense that the latter is based on the development of a state of social powerlessness isomorphic to religious abstraction of power to the theoretic level. Religious knowledge is a revolutionary change from magic because the type of thinking and conception of power is quite different; but, when this revolution occurs, the society has already developed a separation in power and a division of mental and physical labor. Religion, therefore, does not offer a political or social change, but tends to maintain (and be isomorphic to) the present by focusing attention on the abstract. In this sense it may be referred to as an opiate. But religion is isomorphic to social structure, and it is not a question of the knowledge system reflecting a social structure which is somehow its cause. The relationship is not a causal relationship between material and ideal conditions but a question of the mutual coexistence of isomorphic structures.

Weber noted that "By themselves, the masses . . . have everywhere remained engulfed in the massive and archaic growth of magic—unless a prophecy that holds out specific promises has swept them into a religious movement."[62] The theory of knowledge views magic as the earliest form of knowledge isomorphic to the simplest social structures. The development of more complex structures may not significantly change the lives of the ordinary individuals, and the complexity introduced may not consist of anything more than a centrality of communication necessitated by the combination of a set of agrarian tribes. In the simplest cases, tribal life was little effected with the relationship to the central power consisting of little more than the payment of taxes. Under these conditions the central group was made up of warriors whose military specialization allowed them to maintain power over the tribes. If the central power is able to defend its territory, the devastation can be eliminated which might otherwise have resulted from war between the tribes. This results in an increase in general wealth which then becomes available to the ruling group. When ruling groups can be maintained with little or no more income than that saved by military stabilization, then the lot of the majority has not been much effected. The increased wealth is not diffused in the tribes, and little change has occurred in the average individual's life. Under such conditions, the intensity of internal administration is very low, and the transformation from independent tribal member to lower class position in an empire has little effect upon the average individual, particularly in rural areas. Consequently, magic would still prevail. (Even today peasants in rural areas in France remain magical in orientation, although nominally Catholic.) Such conditions were consciously fostered by the mandarins throughout their history in China. Weber ob-

[62] Weber, *Essays*, p. 277.

served that the intensity of administration there was so low that the extended family, a continuation of the tribe, did most or all of the governing at the local level. The fiscal policy of the mandarins consistently attempted to reduce power differentials among the masses and to avoid their complete impoverishment. The continuation of these conditions tended to maintain the magical tradition successfully up to modern times.

The internal conditions of the Roman Empire however were quite different. It was characterized by the manorial system and a highly intensive administration with central tax gathering. The establishment of the manorial system considerably transformed the conditions of life for most of the inhabitants of the areas in which it was introduced by the Romans. When the native inhabitants of a region were conquered, they were either enslaved or were displaced from the land and slaves imported. The lives of the slaves within the manor were intensively regulated, and they lived at bare subsistence. The combination of such exploitation and some technological advancements created wealth in the form of grain, oil, meat, or other commodities which was not consumed by the manor but sold in the cities for the profit of the manor owner. The factory was the urban equivalent of the manor, having a primitive division of labor and supporting its owner by the exploitation of slaves. Independent small land owners and free craftsmen could compete against these structures only by reducing their own standards of living to the lowest possible levels.

While introducing these economic transformations, the Roman state consistently expanded its taxation and administrative capabilities. To the average citizen, the extension of Roman law meant impoverishment because it was accompanied by the tax collector. These taxes supported a huge army and administrative officials of diverse ranks and led to a greater polarization of stratification than that existing at any previous time in history. The large manor owners and higher officials close to the Emperor formed an extremely wealthy class, while at the other extreme were slaves and the free urban proletariat who were often unemployed or employed at the lowest possible wages because of their competition with the slave system.

The slaves and urban proletariat were transformed from the conditions of their previous tribal existence where all competed for a relatively small distribution of power, to conditions of powerlessness confronted by a degree of central power never before experienced. The powerless conditions of life no longer fit the ideas of magical knowledge but were isomorphic to religion. The invention of religious ideas at this time was in a climate well suited for its reception. Weber noted that religion has been a substitute for magic.[63] But this is true only in the sense discussed above. Religion may take the

---

[63] See *ibid.*, p. 274.

place of magic, but only to the extent that the conditions of existence of those involved have been transformed. When such a transformation has not taken place, it will be accepted only if it can be modified to fit into the existing magical system of knowledge, and magic will prevail.

The *creation* of religious theology is dependent upon the development of relatively powerless mental laborers. In Roman times those who spread and systematized the ideas of prophecies were from such a group. Christianity succeeded in competition with other prophecies because it was most purely a religion and most closely fit the conditions of existence created by the Empire.

The conditions of life of the ruling class and wealthy groups of the Empire, however, were isomorphic to the maintenance of magical knowledge. The power held from Julius Caesar onward was such that, while religious cults grew up around the favored groups, they were given magical interpretation by the Emperor and the highest status groups. Nevertheless this power became even more centralized and, from the time of Tiberius onward, was mainly concentrated in the hands of the Emperor himself; other positions thus became increasingly tenuous. A succession of emperors held power so completely and absolutely that they were conceived as deities (even sometimes by themselves, and often prior to their deaths). This behavior has been described as mad by modern historians, but it can be explained as a result of this ultimate concentration of worldly power.

The concentration of power in the hands of the Emperor meant that conditions isomorphic to magical knowledge held only for that one person. The lives of the higher status groups became so precariously dependent upon the behavior of the Emperor that they were, in effect, powerless. Even these groups achieved conditions of existence conducive to adoption of religion. Nevertheless, the fate of these upper status groups and that of the Emperor was closely tied with the continued success of the Empire. The Empire, however, could not succeed indefinitely because the manorial-slavery system depended on the continual use of slaves who did not reproduce themselves. Their replenishment required constant expansion of boundaries, but the Empire reached a point beyond which it was unable to expand. This culminated in the breakdown of the manorial system into what eventually became the feudal system.

The feudal system, however, did not yield the same amount of surplus wealth because it somewhat reduced exploitation. Rome's economic base contracted and with it the size of the armies. This lack of general success reduced the power of the Emperor and upper status groups, transforming their conditions of existence to such an extent that they fit a religious knowledge system better than magic. The adoption of the Christian religion by Constantine was followed by its adoption by those higher status groups who had held out until that time. Finally Christianity became the dominant system of knowledge of the Empire.

COMPLEX RELIGIOUS STRUCTURES

Magic attributes the causes of specific action to the power of individuals or objects involved, but religion drains the world of power. The explanation of how actions occur in the absence of power is a basic problem of theology. There is only one purely religious solution to this problem: if the world is powerless, all earthly happenings must occur at the instigation of a non-worldly power-concept—a god. The relations between this power-concept and empirical objects, including men, are authority relations. The explanation of all events is in terms of the conception of the action of this power-concept. Aquinas' proof of the existence of God (which he borrowed from Aristotle) represents one expression of this idea. He argued that all events have causes, and those causes have prior causes, which have prior causes, while nevertheless an infinity of causes is impossible; therefore, he concluded, there must have been a first cause, and that is God. This view neatly solves the problem of action in this world by tracing it back to its original source in an unbroken chain of power. God, the unmoved mover, the power-concept, is ultimately responsible for all action.

Leibniz presented what was perhaps an even more purely religious explanation. He regarded empirical things as entirely unrelated to one another, but related only to God. The superficial appearance of relatedness of empirical things is merely a reflection of God's consistency. This notion is illustrated by two clocks, one running slightly ahead of the other. The first one strikes the hour first, and then the other strikes; and this action is repeated over and over again. But the striking of the second clock was not caused by the first, although these events occurred side by side and the one took place immediately prior to the other. All empirical occurrences are believed to proceed in this manner. The appearance of direct connection of events occurring in temporal proximity is only a superficial impression and is false.

Few theologies have maintained the pure conception that all empirical happenings are a direct consequence of their relation to the power-concept because of the evident contradiction with the need for the religious man to follow the ethical demands of that power-concept. The interjection of free will allows man at least a minimum of power and reestablishes empirical connection. Under these conditions, some happenings are not seen as the direct or immediate responsibility of the power-concept. Yet empirical actions can be explained by connection to the god-concept when convenient.

The actions of men which can be explained by god's authority are those which conform to the ethic. In the simplest case in which the division of labor is small, everyone must know what the ethic is and guide actions accordingly. These conditions were characteristic of early Christianity, Protestant ascetic sects, and early Mohammedanism. But when the division of labor is more complex, the social structure and relationship to the god-concept is different.

The development of religious organization means that there will be positions specializing in knowledge of the theology and ethic. When positions are developed which specialize in religious knowledge, other positions are left dependent upon them as adherents to the religion. This separation divides the priesthood from the laity; and, when it is carried to an extreme as in Catholicism, religious knowledge is almost completely appropriated by the priesthood while the laity are left to their faith. The first consequence of the separation of the laity from religious knowledge is ritual action. Ritual is habitual in form and effectively devoid of subjective meaning, but it is the only religious observance possible to those who have no religious knowledge. Of course, the religious conception of powerlessness can lead to the adoption of ritual by those who are not separated from religious knowledge. On the other hand, as in the case of the Quakers, where there is no division of labor there is no ritual.

Complex religious structures are governed by authority relations. In the Catholic Church the authority of God over the Pope is reflected in the authority of the Pope over the Cardinals, and so on, down to the authority of the priests over the laymen. The Pope is closest to the power source, while the laymen are farthest removed from God. The Pope has greatest authority while the layman has least. The authority position of any individual is determined by his position in the hierarchy of authority leading to God.

Questions of theology and ethics are always decided by those of greater authority in the hierarchy because of their closer position to the god-concept. The laity are separated both from knowledge of theology and of ethics, and they are consequently unable to understand or interpret them. They will necessarily err in their actions and will have to be corrected. Their errors will accumulate; and, to avoid wholesale damnation of the laity, the concept of "grace" must be introduced. Salvation can thus be guaranteed through the proper relationship to the hierarchy. This advantage also has the attractive result that the hierarchy is simultaneously guaranteed social control over the laity.

In practice, the interposition of the hierarchy between the individual and his god-concept has meant that he becomes unable to fulfill ethical demands by himself, nor even (from the viewpoint of the hierarchy) to understand them. The individual at the bottom of the hierarchy, although he may be a member of a religious organization, does not himself have any knowledge of the knowledge system he accepts, and he will have to be instructed by the officials of the hierarchy. But, according to Weber:

> the perpetual control of an individual's life pattern by the official, whether father confessor or spiritual director, empowered to distribute grace, a control that in certain respects is very effective, is in practice very often cancelled by the circumstance that there is always grace remaining to be distributed anew. . . . As a consequence, the pattern of everyday life could be influenced by these religions only in the direction of traditionalism.[64]

This is not surprising, since the system of knowledge cannot be expected to effect the layman directly if he does not have effective knowledge of it.

SIMPLE RELIGIOUS STRUCTURES

In the absence of hierarchy, the layman is directly related to his god-concept. His behavior is dependent upon his own religious knowledge, and the theology and ethic must consequently be much simpler and be accessible to all. Historically this has been accomplished in two ways. In early Mohammedanism knowledge was spread by means of an oral tradition, while in early Christianity it was spread by the written word. The emphasis on the *Bible* as the only authoritative word of God in Protestantism was not accidental. The elimination of the hierarchy required a great simplification of the theology in order for the ordinary man to understand it. The invention of printing greatly facilitated the rise of Protestantism by making the written authority widely available.

The elimination of the hierarchy resulted for the religious man in what Weber called "an acute . . . permanent state of tension in relation to the world and its orders."[65] He observed elsewhere that "The conflict between empirical reality and this conception of the world as a meaningful totality, which is based on a religious postuate, produces the strongest tensions in man's inner life as well as in his external relationship to the world."[66] This results in "an effort to systematize all the manifestations of life."[67] The goal of this behavior is salvation: "We shall designate this type of attitude toward salvation, which is characterized by a methodical procedure for achieving religious salvation, as 'ascetic.'"[68]

Weber viewed salvation as a broad term including both the religious escape from the empirical world and the end point of mystical activity. Salvation for the religious man, however, has a meaning quite different

---

[64] Weber, *Religion*, p. 189.
[65] Weber, *Essays*, p. 328.
[66] Weber, *Religion*, p. 59.
[67] *Ibid.*, p. 59.
[68] *Ibid.*, p. 164.

from that of the mystic. For the religious man, salvation is the escape of his rationally conceived soul to a rationally conceived other world. The means of that escape are determined by the theology and ethic of his religion. His behavior is governed by reference to theoretic ideas, and "rational asceticism" here refers to the methodical orientation of behavior to a theological and ethical system. In other words, he who actually governs his behavior by the religious system is a rational asceticist. The previous development of theoretic ideas is a necessary condition for such action, and Weber described rational asceticism as a result of ethical prophecy; however, he pointed out, individuals involved in religious organizations are not always rational asceticists.

Rational asceticism requires acquaintance with the theology and ethic of a religious system of knowledge. The separation of religious behavior from worldly behavior is what Weber called "other-worldly asceticism." Monks or other members of a religious hierarchy are separated in such cases from the laity and supported by them. The separation of the laity from acquaintance with the rational contents of the system of knowledge makes rational asceticism impossible for them. Because of the isolation of religious knowledge–holders from the average man, such asceticism cannot have much effect on other social relations. Nevertheless, rational asceticism may be common to all members of a religious group if (1) its knowledge is purely religious, (2) the theological and ethical systems are simple, (3) the division of religious labor is minimal, and (4) their conditions of life will support asceticism.

If the knowledge system is not purely religious, if perhaps it is a mixture of magic and religion, then thought will not be rational and abstractive, and rational asceticism is impossible. If the theology and ethical systems are too complex, only full time application to them will lead to understanding, and only a few will be able to master them while others provide support for those few. If religious labor is divided, some must be ignorant of the system and incapable of rationality. Finally, if social conditions are such that individuals are inclined to participate in worldly pleasures (especially if they live above the level of subsistence), there would be no social basis for their acceptance of the system of knowledge.

Only under these conditions can rational asceticism be brought out of the monestary and into activities which are not separated from political and economic concerns. As Weber pointed out, early Protestant sects eliminated hierarchy and the division of religious labor. Compared with Catholicism, Protestant theology and ethics were radically simplified, usually by viewing only the *Bible* as inspired. Inexpensive printing allowed the dissemination of the contents of the *Bible* to all members of the religious organizations of the Protestant sects.

Weber noted that the basic techniques of modern industrial capitalism had already been established under monopoly conditions before the Reformation. A money economy also existed based on commercial and finance capitalism. But these conditions did not involve the great mass of the people of Europe. In fact, the involvement of more than a narrow stratum in capitalism required the development of industry. But the development of industry required huge investments of capital, and in a free market there was no assurance that profit would follow. Who would invest great amounts in industry and keep reinvesting in the same undertaking in spite of the constant pressure of free competition? Investment in such a venture would be judged today as bad economic policy.

The rational asceticist, however, was not concerned with good economic policy but with the salvation of his soul. For the early capitalist entrepreneur operating in a free market, wealth was not created to be taken out of the enterprise. Those who did not reinvest, unless they controlled their market, were forced out by more efficient capitalists who did reinvest. The conditions of existence of the early capitalist therefore fit rational asceticism. In fact, the beginnings of industrial capitalism created conditions conducive to the maintenance of asceticism, while religion provided the rationalism necessary for the further development and spread of capitalism. There was an isomorphism between social conditions and type of knowledge system.

Once industrial capitalism gained its first success, however, the bourgeoisie achieved political power and, with it, control over markets. Furthermore, since the outcome of their competition was monopoly, there was no longer any pressure toward asceticism. In the words of John Wesley:

> I fear, wherever riches have increased, the essence of religion has decreased in the same proportion. Therefore I do not see how it is possible, in the nature of things, for any revival of true religion to continue long. For religion must necessarily produce both industry and frugality, and these cannot but produce riches. But as riches increase, so will pride, anger, and love of the world in all its branches. How then is it possible that Methodism, that is, a religion of the heart, though it flourishes now as a green bay tree, should continue in this state? For the Methodists in every place grow diligent and frugal; consequently they increase in goods. Hence they proportionately increase in pride, in anger, in the desire of the flesh, the desire of the eyes, and the pride of life. So, although the form of religion remains, the spirit is swiftly vanishing away. Is there no way to prevent this—this continual decay of pure religion? We ought not to prevent people from being diligent and frugal; *we must exhort all Christians to gain all they can, and to save all they can; that is, in effect, to grow rich.*[69]

In other words, the social conditions of the successful bourgeoisie were

---

[69] Quoted in Max Weber, *The Protestant Ethic and the Spirit of Capitalism*, trans. by T. Parsons (New York: Charles Scribner's, 1958), p. 175.

isomorphic to magic, not to religion. They were "Specialists without spirit, sensualists without heart; this nullity imagines that it has attained a level of civilization never before achieved."[70]

Once the bourgeoisie attained worldly power, they were able to control the life conditions of the proletariat; and, in spite of increasing riches, the proletariat remained impoverished and in conditions conducive to religion.

[70] *Ibid.*, p. 182.

CHAPTER SIX

THE MYSTIC
REACTION

It is a mistake to think of mysticism as religion. The two share almost no positive characteristics. There are no congregations of mystics, no churches of mysticism, and no mystic preachers. Mysticism needs no sacred places, no icons, crosses, or sacred objects. Mysticism has no theology. In fact, very little of mysticism can be communicated at all. Mysticism and religion do not even have similar results. In certain social conditions religion can transform the world, but mysticism never can. Mysticism knows no holy wars. The only social effect mysticism can have is negative. Mysticism is, as Nietzsche pointed out, beyond good and evil.

Mysticism and religion do, however, share one negative characteristic, and this may be the source of the confusion made between them. Both offer escape from the empirical and from the consequences of magic. Magical knowledge based solely on empirical connection has shaky foundations which become obvious as thinking becomes more sophisticated: under some conditions empirical connection will fail, and empirical generalization will not hold up. The expansion of society tends to drain magical power away from most of its members into central positions, reducing the legitimization of the notion of power for all. The religious solution is a transvaluation, rejecting the magical conception of power in favor of abstract power, and rejecting empirical connection in favor of rational connection.

The mystical solution is quite different. Confronted with the drain of power through social relations, the mystic rigorously limits his social relations. He replaces an empirical conception of power with an abstractive one. Instead of attempting to understand and control the empirical world, he accepts it as it appears to him, but rejects its goals. He rejects the search for power in the world as a distraction from his abstract end. Social relations with those who seek magical power only increase his distraction. The mystic attempts to retreat from worldly concerns. Mysticism is a rebellion against what is; the mystic accepts what he sees as real, but he does not like what he sees and wishes to escape from it.

Mysticism can also be a reaction against religion. The mystic does not concern himself with theological arguments but views the acceptance of a theology to be equally as self-defeating as magic. The mystic is not concerned with rational connection. From his point of view the ultimate result of rational connection is paradox, and the religious man wastes his time in futile reasoning.

Both magic and religion are types of knowledge upon which solid social organizations have been built; but mysticism, although associated with definite social conditions, is asocial. In a magical system, the balance of power is worked out in social relations. In a religious system, individuals apply ethical rules to social behavior and discuss, teach, and learn theology. Mysticism has none of these. The magical individual engages in power relations and the religious man is involved in authority relations. No equivalent of either exists for the mystic. In fact, the only basis for social relations is the set of rules the mystic follows to attain his abstract end, but these rules require retreat from social relations and will not support social organization of any complexity. These rules exist only in order to allow others to attempt to attain mystical abstract goals, and a mystical system of knowledge is never the sole support of social organization.

A mystical system of knowledge combines empirical and abstractive thinking. The mystic makes connections between observables in his thinking and connects them to some abstract concept at the theoretic level. However, since this abstract concept is not logically or systematically connected to others, mysticism does not make rational connections. The abstract concept is equivalent to the mystical notion of power. Power is to be found by directing one's goals toward an abstract concept, not toward a rational concept as in religion or toward an empirical goal as in magic.

In its earliest form Buddhism was a remarkably pure example of mysticism. In contrast to religion, which teaches that the world is sinful and that the purpose of human life is to escape to a rationally conceived heaven, Buddhism taught that the world is neither good nor evil and should be observed for what it *is*, but man should not depend on it. Christian salvation involves the notion of getting from what is sinful to what is good, while *Nirvana* is the escape from what is to what is not.

Buddhism did not include a notion of an otherworldly god; but it did not, on the other hand deny it:

Buddhism has no God, it has not even the vague and confused notion of a Universal Spirit, in which, according to orthodox Brahmanism and the Sankhya, the human soul is absorbed. Neither does it admit nature properly so called, and it does not make the great distinction between the spirit and the material world which is the system and glory of Kapila; lastly, it confuses man with his earthly surroundings, even while it preaches virtue to him. It cannot, therefore, unite the human soul, which it never even mentions, either to a God whom it does not know, or to nature which it ignores.[1]

It is, in fact, contrary to Buddhist behavior to possess or deny rational concepts. "In reality, Buddhism is no more 'atheistical' than it is 'theistic' or 'pantheistic'; . . . it does not place itself at the point of view where these terms have any meaning."[2] In other words, it does not utilize or recognize rational thought connection. Other metaphysical concepts and arguments, such as salvation, are also disregarded:

> If you desire a next life and there is a next life, you have no problem. If you desire a next life and there is no next life, you will be frustrated. If you desire no next life and there is no next life, you have no problem. If you desire no next life and there is a next life, you will be frustrated. In either case, whether there is or is not a next life, you will be frustrated if you want what will not be. Hence, so far as happiness is concerned, the important issue is not whether there is or is not a next life, but whether or not you are willing to accept things as they will be, however they will be.[3]

The Buddhist conception of an attitude toward the world becomes a systematic empiricism in its denial of the relevance of metaphysical speculation and argument. Happiness is to be achieved in the present life and *Nirvana* (the highest wisdom) is to be achieved by seeing things as they are.[4] Life, according to Guatama, is full of suffering: "I only teach two things, O disciples: suffering (*duhkha*) and release from suffering."[5] Suffering results from ignorance, from man's craving for *what he is not.*[6] Happiness results from seeing the world as it is and thus not desiring what cannot be obtained. Man tends to cling to his ego, and, in doing so, increases his anxiety and ties himself to his petty cravings. In doing so, he also ties himself to the Wheel of Existence.

But Buddhism, although it emphasizes empirical observation, is not magical. Man must know the world as it is, not to gain ends within it, but

---

[1] J. Barthelemy Saint-Hilaire, *Life and Legend of Buddha,* trans. by L. Ensor (Calcutta: Susil Gupta, 1957), p. 87.

[2] Floyd H. Ross, *The Meaning of Life in Hinduism and Buddhism* (London: Routledge & Kegan Paul, 1952), p. 80.

[3] A. J. Bahm, *Philosophy of the Buddha* (New York: Harper & Brothers, 1958), p. 19.

[4] See Charles Eliot, *Hinduism and Buddhism: An Historical Sketch* (London: Routledge & Kegan Paul, 1962), p. xxi.

[5] Ross, *Hinduism and Buddhism,* p. 85.

[6] See *ibid.,* p. 88.

to escape from dependence on it. To obtain *Nirvana*, man renounces his ego and his craving for worldly things. He must follow the Eightfold Path to knowledge:

1. through "right view": "He must look into his own existence and see the facts of suffering for what they are;"[7]
2. through "right aspiration": "the resolve to renounce sensual pleasures, the resolve to have malice toward none, and the resolve to harm no living creatures ... [in] ... the hope to live in love with all;"[8]
3. through "right speech": "abstaining from falsehood, backbiting, harsh language and frivolous talk;"[9]
4. through "right behavior": "to abstain from destroying life, taking what is not given ... Not to kill, steal, lie, be unchaste, or drink intoxicants;"[10]
5. through "right livelihood": choosing "a calling which will not force him to do things injurious to other human beings, human or subhuman, or to his own spiritual growth;"[11]
6. through "right effort": "the control of the passions;"[12]
7. through "right mindfulness": "Instead of viewing things through the distorted spectacles of craving, one must learn to see things as they are;"[13]
8. through "right contemplation": described by Guatama, "I have been alone in rapture of thought ... till I rose above perception of the world without, into an infinite space of cognition, and this again melted into nothing ... Insight came, and I discerned with the celestial vision the way of the world, the tendencies of men, and their coming to be, past, present, and yet to come."[14]

The achievement of this eighth step is *Nirvana*, the highest wisdom. The essence of the Eightfold Path is consistent and simple: accept the things of the world as they are, do not allow your mind to distort them, do not harm them, and seek true wisdom in contemplation.

In spite of the various warnings about the deceptions of the senses, the Eightfold Path describes empirical ethical rules, with the final step being the lifting of the mind, abstraction from reality to the theoretic level. Religion, however, consists of the abstraction of theoretic concepts to the empirical world, while Buddhism consists of the reverse. True existence is at the empirical level, and *Nirvana* is found in the present by a mental elevation of the perception of the world as it is. While Buddhism is not religious, neither is it magical, for it does not consist of purely empirical thinking and rejects the notion of magical power. The goal of Buddhism is the abstraction

---

[7] *Ibid.*, p. 108.
[8] *Ibid.*, p. 108.
[9] *Ibid.*, p. 111.
[10] *Ibid.*, p. 111.
[11] *Ibid.*, p. 112.
[12] *Ibid.*, p. 112.
[13] *Ibid.*, p. 113.
[14] *Ibid.*, p. 114.

of the empirical to the theoretic level, unlike magic in which goals are many and are all empirical. Thus, power in Buddhism consists in getting from the observational level to the theoretic level. It consists of taking the world for what it is and thus being free from it and not depending on it.

If Nietzsche had been consistent in his magical orientation, he should have opposed Buddhist mysticism as well as Christianity. He did call both 'nihilistic' which, in his terms, means that both reject power.[15] But there are other reasons why mysticism is more appealing than religion from the viewpoint of magical knowledge. "The concept of 'God' had long been disposed of when it arrived."[16] . . . "Buddhism is a hundred times more realistic than Christianity,"[17] (probably because it has an empirical component) . . . "*Prayer* is ruled out, and so is *asceticism*; there is no categorical imperitive, no *compulsion* whatever."[18] . . . "In the Buddha's doctrine, egoism becomes a duty: the 'one thing needful,' the question 'how can *you* escape from suffering?' regulates and limits the whole spiritual diet."[19] Because it has no moral concepts, mysticism stands "*beyond* good and evil."[20]

Nietzsche's thinking is actually consistent. The individual who accepts a magical system of knowledge should view mysticism as preferable to religion, if only because it does not offer a theology which is contrary to magic. Mysticism, like magic, accepts empirical thinking. It differs in that it rejects empirical goals.

Weber classified Buddhism in the same category as Christianity, Islam, and Judaism, as a religion. This is an error which might have been expected because of his failure to formally define religion. He, nevertheless, noted that mysticism has empirical manifestations which are quite distinctive. Much of his concern was oriented to the role of religion in the promotion of rationalism:

> The most irrational form of religious behavior, the mystic experience, is in its innermost being not only alien but hostile to all form. Form is unfortunate and inexpressible to the mystic because he believes precisely in the experience which lies beyond any kind of determination and form. For him the indubitable psychological affinity of profoundly shaking experiences in art and religion can only be a symptom of the diabolical nature of art.[21]

Here Weber's reference to mysticism as irrational fits the view that it lacks

[15] See Friedrich Nietzsche, *The Portable Nietzsche*, selected and trans. by Walter Kaufmann (New York: The Viking Press, 1954), p. 586.

[16] *Ibid.*, pp. 586–87.

[17] *Ibid.*, p. 586.

[18] *Ibid.*, p. 587.

[19] *Ibid.*, p. 588.

[20] *Ibid.*, p. 587.

[21] Max Weber, *From Max Weber: Essays in Sociology*, trans. by H.H. Gerth and C.W. Mills (New York: Oxford University Press, 1958), p. 342.

rational connection of concepts at the theoretic level, but elsewhere he noted that mysticism

> must originally be associated with a considerable degree of systematically rationalized patterning of life. Only this, indeed, leads to concentration upon the boon of salvation. Yet, rationalization is only an instrument for attaining the goal of contemplation and is of an essentially negative type, consisting of the avoidance of interruptions caused by nature and the social milieu.[22]

Weber's two statements appear contradictory: either mysticism is irrational or it is rational. The confusion arises from the fact that Weber defined two types of rationalism which were not distinguished in these contexts. Mysticism is irrational in that it makes no conceptual connections, and it is rational in that it makes empirical connections (purposive rationality). As far as these observations go, they agree with the view of mysticism given here by the theory of knowledge. There is recognition of the empirical component and the lack of rational connection, but there is no conception of abstractive connection.

Weber refers to the founder of a mystical system of knowledge as an exemplary prophet: "Exemplary prophecy points out the path to salvation by exemplary living."[23] The exemplary prophet "by his personal example, demonstrates to others the way to . . . salvation."[24] This type of prophecy "says nothing about a divine mission or an ethical duty of obedience, but rather directs itself to the self-interest of those who crave salvation, recommending to them the same path as he himself traversed."[25] According to Weber, this type is particularly characteristic of India (especially of Buddha) but also includes Lao Tzu in China.

It should be remembered that "salvation" was a very broad category for Weber, including the desire to escape from the empirical. In that sense, but not in the narrower sense of the Western-Christian notion of salvation, mysticism offers salvation, an escape from the world as it is empirically apprehended. But this salvation is logically and substantively unlike religious salvation. Religious salvation offers a new life in a rationally conceived

---

[22] Max Weber, *The Sociology of Religion*, trans. by E. Fischoff (Boston: Beacon Press, 1964), p. 170.

[23] Weber, *Essays*, p. 285. In comparing the two types of prophecy Weber noted that "The most varied transitions and combinations are found between the polar opposites . . . They have been historical rather than logical or even psychological constructions without contradiction." (p. 291) It is certainly true that empirical cases have been mixed, but the implication that they can only be understood historically demonstrates the limits to Weber's approach to scientific explanation. Offering a scientific explanation for an event is quite different from providing a descriptive account of it.

[24] Weber, *Religion*, p. 55.

[25] *Ibid.*, p. 55.

world which, although its exact character is not known, offers a life in which the soul has similar experiences to those on earth. This salvation is attained at death when the soul, the rationally conceived essence of life, departs from the body or is taken by the god-concept.

Mystical salvation is completely different. It is not obtained after death but during life. It is not attained as a consequence of the notion of action of a god-concept, but instead it must be obtained by the individual during his worldly life by definite means. In a sense, the relationship between death and salvation is reversed: in religion death is followed by salvation, but in mysticism salvation (or total extinction of empirical desires) leads to death. The mystic's goal is not empirical death because that would be a projection of an empirical goal. Once one has lifted oneself above the empirical, the end has been achieved, and further empirical existence is without meaning.

The exemplary prophet is no more magical than the ethical prophet. Certainly the power of the exemplary prophet is somewhat more personal than that of the ethical prophet in that he has the ability to lift himself above the empirical; but, precisely for this reason, his power is not empirical (or magical) but abstractive. This characterizes a third type of charisma which is neither the charismatic power of the magician nor the charismatic authority of the ethical prophet, theologian, or priest. It is charismatic *individualism* in which the successful mystic has personal charisma, but he is not engaged in structured social relations. He is not a magician and does not have empirical power over others, nor is he a religious man with authority over others. He possesses charisma of his own without domination over others or subordination to others.

The relationship between an exemplary prophet and the mystics who follow him is quite different from that between the ethical prophet and religious ascetics. In the latter case theoretic ideas need to have been previously rationalized by theologians. Only then can that system be applied and can asceticism exist. Between the ascetic and the prophet is the theologian with his task of systematization. Moreover, the ascetic and his prophet behave quite differently. The ascetic may do as the prophet says, but he does not do as the prophet does.

No systematization stands between the mystic and his prophet who is himself a mystic and has worked out a method of attaining an abstract goal. The method is the major content of what the exemplary prophet says, and the intent is not so much to do as the prophet *says* but to do as he *does*. If the followers are to do exactly as their prophet does, there is less division of labor in mysticism than in even the simplest religious traditions. In fact, there is no division of mental labor because there are no rational connections made in a mystical system. The mystic's abstractive goal by its very nature is to be obtained only by individual effort; therefore, there is no way that the labor can be divided. Although some mystics may be more concerned with their own salvation while others are more concerned with teaching others, this is a division of emphasis rather than a division of labor. Mystics are both individuals concerned with the escape from the empirical and teachers by their example.

Because mysticism has no division of labor, it has no basis for the development of centrality, and therefore, no organization. Mysticism has no theology and no need for theologians. In the pure case it has neither laity nor priests nor preachers. Since it lacks rationalized authority, hierarchy cannot be established. The pure empirical case of ancient Buddhism, as Weber pointed out, had no hierarchical organization whatsoever.[26] A lack of hierarchy may also be found in Sūfism and other comparatively pure cases of this type of system.

Both mysticism and religion offer an escape from the empirical because both have an abstractive component, but here their similarity ends. The two may develop, however, in answer to the same empirical problem— powerlessness and consequent suffering—Both offer solutions to this problem which transcend empiricism. They are consequently put into the same category and thought to be interchangeable but their interchangeability is limited to this shared characteristic alone. The basic similarity in roles of reaction to magical power means that they may be alternative courses of change in some situations. The adoption of one or the other reaction will depend upon its compatibility with the social structure.

In the absence of rational connection, only one type of escape from the empirical is possible, according to the theory of knowledge, and that is mysticism. Northrop claimed that the crucial difference between East and West was precisely that Eastern thought has lacked the theoretic component while Western thought has made much use of it.[27] The explanation of the rise of mysticism or religion, however, cannot be made by making an empirical generalization about the difference between East and West as Northrop has done. This distinction is limited in scope to these two regions and, like all generalizations, there are exceptions to it. It is nevertheless historically accurate to state that the theoretic component has been more in use in the West than in the East. In China the theoretic component seems to have been essentially absent. Chinese civilization was in many ways similar to the culture of primitive communities in spite of the existence of some literate officials and a much larger territory. The similarities include: the charismatic power of the emperor and its direct connection to success; the

---

[26] See *ibid.*, p. 73.
[27] See F.S.C. Northrop, *The Meeting of East and West* (New York: The Macmillan Company, 1953), pp. 294–302.

continued isolation and high level of ethnocentrism; the primitive form of writing; the simple, though geographically extensive, political structure; the primitive legal structure; and familialism. These attributes are associated more often with primitive communities than with great empires.

Northrop maintains that the lack of the theoretic component is the explanation for the difference between China and the West. Lacking the theoretic component, Chinese thought was not subject to either rational extension or revolution as Western thought was; therefore, it should have changed little from its beginnings. Confucius claimed to be saying nothing more than what was contained in ancient tradition which, through him, was subsequently maintained.[28] One should therefore be able to trace the reliance on empirical thought back to primitive Chinese cultures, but there are no records of these cultures.

Assuming the similarity of Chinese culture to that of primitive communities, we can account for certain facts. For instance, the Chinese conception of the basis of social life and the root of civilization is the cultivation of personal life.[29] If all men were cultivated, they could lead perfect lives. As their lives became perfected, so would civilization and the empire. Nominalism and individualism of this sort have been associated with empiricism in the West. To the nominalist, the idea of social structure is a mystery, and the effects of its change cannot be planned. It follows that such change might be dangerous and should be avoided. Old ways are regarded as safest. The traditionalism of Chinese culture, it may be argued, follows as a consequence of its dependence upon empirical thinking. The atheism of Confucianism and the purer forms of Taoism may also be attributed to this type of thought, but such a claim requires more explanation than Northrop offered.

In the eighteenth century Yuan Yuan wrote:

> Our ancients sought phenomena, and ignored theoretical explanation. Since the arrival of the Europeans, the question has always been concerning explanations, circular orbits, eclipses, and squares . . . [but] really it does not seem to me the least inconvenient to ignore the western theoretical explanations and simply consider the facts.[30]

In seeming contradiction to this empirical thinking are the technical accomplishments of the Chinese: printing, gunpowder, the escapement, the magnet, and many more. These developments do not necessarily contradict a traditionalistic conception of Chinese culture and, although far in advance of those in the West, were not a consequence of theoretical science, as the

---

[28] See *ibid.*, pp. 322–46.

[29] See *ibid.*, p. 323.

[30] Quoted in Stephen F. Mason, *A History of the Sciences* (New York: Collier Books, 1962), p. 88.

advances in the West have been over the last 250 years. Moreover, their effects on the Chinese were much less than they later were in Europe. Printing, for example, was invented in China but was not utilized extensively there, whereas it spread throughout Europe in little more than a decade after its introduction. The differential effects of other inventions have also been noted. Both the mode of their development and their comparatively small use make sense if Chinese thought is viewed as empirical.

There are two conditions necessary for the rise of rational connection: the division of mental from manual labor and the development of a phonetically written language. The first was present in China, but the latter was never developed and rational connection was therefore impossible. In the absence of rational thought, religion could not develop, and magical thought remained in China in spite of complex social development. Only one escape from empirical power was possible under these conditions, and that was mysticism.

Chinese thought showed remarkable continuity in its development. With the development of central government and the separation of mental from manual labor, power was partially drained from the less central, lower status positions. Under these conditions, religion or mysticism would be expected to develop; but, in the absence of rational connection, only mysticism was found, not as an internal development but as Buddhism imported from India.

Although theoretic thought was developed in India, nearly everyone but the highest castes maintained a magical system of knowledge. The arrangement of the castes according to the concepts of dharma and karma resulted in an overall social structure quite different from that of primitive society. However, these concepts were simply the basis of arrangement of the castes and did not affect thinking within them. Buddhism was a reaction against Hinduism and magic. Buddha's aim was to escape from the Wheel of Existence, the eternal wheel of rebirth. The Hindu notion of the soul was of an eternal soul which was born and reborn again. Each life allowed the individual an opportunity to gain or lose power accumulated in the present life; but Buddhism viewed continuous rebirth after rebirth as ultimately futile. For the Buddhist, the notion of rebirth was based on a hunger for life. If the hunger for life could be extinguished, then future rebirth might be avoided. The purpose of the Eightfold Path was to escape from the eternal empirical struggle for power imposed on man by the notion of continuous rebirth.[31]

The basic structure of mystical thought is the same everywhere, regard-

---

[31] Hinduism itself offered escape from the cycle of rebirths; however, this escape was limited to those in the highest caste, the Brahmans. There seems to be some uncertainty as to when this development took place. If it were before Buddha, then Buddhism represents a democratization of mysticism. If it were after, it was certainly borrowed.

less of the tradition in which it developed. Thus, although Sūfism was a reaction to a relatively pure religion rather than a reaction to magic, its structure is like that of ancient Buddhism. This does not mean that the content of Sūfism is expected to be identical to that of Buddhism; there is no reason why the content should be similar except as it is conditioned by the formal thought structure. When it is similar, the similarity is expected to be by analogy, the similar structuring of different ideas.

"The fundamental tenets [of the Sūfis] are that nothing exists absolutely but God, that the human soul is an emanation from his essences."[32] God, according to this belief, is diffused over the universe which presents itself in its empirical form as "a world of delusion."[33] The aim of the Sūfi is not action in the world, but union with God, "To be reabsorbed into the glorious essence of God."[34]

The Sūfis believe that "sense and reason cannot transcend phenomena or see the real Being which underlies them all, so sense and reason must be ignored and superseded in favour of the 'inner light.' "[35] Thus it follows that, to the Sūfis, "phenomenal existence is conceived of as a veil, which conceals the truth from man's view."[36]

In order to escape from phenomenal existence and so attain unity with the Divine, it is first necessary to escape from self.[37] "Self is at once the primal source of suffering and sin."[38] The escape from self as the source of suffering is comparable to the Buddhist denial of ego as the source of craving and thus suffering.

The path of annihilation of self in the unity with God has eight stages:

1. service
2. love, which, when it has expelled all earthly desires, leads to
3. seclusion which involves contemplation, resulting in
4. knowledge
5. ecstacy
6. true knowledge of the God
7. union with the God
8. personal extinction.[39]

Like the eight steps to *Nirvana* in Buddhism, the aim of the eight stages

[32] Margaret Smith, ed., *The Sūfi Path of Love: An Anthology of Sūfism* (London: Luzac and Company, Ltd., 1954), p. 1.
[33] *Ibid.*, p. 3.
[34] *Ibid.*, p. 7.
[35] *Ibid.*, p. 6.
[36] *Ibid.*, p. 13.
[37] See *ibid.*, p. 14.
[38] *Ibid.*, p. 14.
[39] See *ibid.*, p. 8.

is clearly to lift the mind out of its concerns in the empirical world into total absorption in the abstract. Nevertheless, this abstraction is through extension of the empirical world:

> The Unique Substance viewed as absolute . . . is the Real (*al-Haqq*). On the other hand, viewed in His aspect of multiplicity and plurality, under which He displays himself when clothed with phenomena, He is the whole created universe. Therefore the universe is the outward visible expression of the Real, and the Real is the inner unseen reality of the Universe.[40]

Sūfism is very like Buddhism in structure. It seeks union with God in a way very similar to the Buddhist search for *Nirvana* by denial of self and consequent emancipation from dependence on the world. Like, Buddhism, but unlike Mohammedanism from which it arose, it ignores the rationalistic connection of theology. "There was, in *their* view, but one way to knowledge—not the rational and second-hand 'knowledge' ('*ilm*) of the schools, but direct and personal 'experience' (*ma'rifa*) culminating in momentary union of absorption into the Godhead. Theology, so far from assisting this process, actually hindered it."[41] Sūfi, then, is not religious, nor is it magical. It is not concerned with theological connections or empirical ends. Although it differs in content somewhat from Buddhism, it is like it in structure. Even the content does not differ significantly; since the concentration is on abstraction, the content is somewhat limited. The Sūfi are concerned with getting from their condition on the observational level to the theoretic level; thought is not fixed at either level. Although Mohammedanism has theology, it is neglected by the Sūfis who attain the equivalent of *Nirvana* by abstraction conceived as union with God. The particular labels of *Nirvana* and "union with God" may seem quite different, but they play identical parts in the structure of thought. Mysticism has the same structure—abstraction from the observational to the theoretic level—whether it is a reaction to magic, as in Buddhism, or a reaction to religion, as in Sūfism.

As Weber pointed out, the "unique character of mystical knowledge consists in the fact that, although it becomes more incommunicable the more strongly it is characterized by idiosyncratic content, it is nevertheless recognized as knowledge."[42] But it is "not . . . knowledge of earthly or heavenly things."[43] Buddhism also rejects speculation; this may be explained by the theory of knowledge. The mystical experience is limited to abstractive connection. Because the experience itself is neither empirical nor rational in its connections, it cannot be explained in terms of either. Since language mean-

---

[40] H.A.R. Gibb, *Mohammedanism* (New York: Oxford University Press, 1962), p. 150.
[41] *Ibid.*, p. 137.
[42] Weber, *Religion*, pp. 169–70.
[43] Max Weber, *The Religion of India*, trans. by H. H. Gerth and Don Martindale (Glencoe: The Free Press, 1958), p. 209.

ings are constructed either empirically or rationally, the mystical experience cannot be put into words. Nevertheless, because it is abstractive, it forms a basis for knowledge. Speculation is rationalistic and is thus rejected as logically opposed to the character of mysticism—mysticism is not concerned with heavenly things. At the same time, the empirical component is accepted, not as a means to empirical ends, but as a means to begin the abstractive process of escape. Thus it is that the monk "who wished to know whether the world was eternal and infinite, and if Buddha would live on after death, was mocked by the master."[44]

Mystical systems of knowledge are never predominant in society because of the structure of their thought. Mysticism is reactionary but does not introduce a program of reform for society; instead, it proposes an escape from it. It is unstructured and has no stratification system based either on power, as in magical systems of knowledge, or on authority, as in religious ones. Because it has no power or authority structure and no center of communication, it cannot handle the problems of a society. It is lack of communication that is important here. The lack of centrality, the complete individualism of mysticism, will not support social organization.

Connected with this lack of centrality for organization is another aspect of mysticism which prevents it from becoming the predominant system of knowledge in a society: since there is no organization in this individualistic system, there is no economic support for it. The mystic does not concern himself with gathering power in the world and is not involved in economic activities; rather, he spends much time in contemplation. Unlike the priest who is supported by his organization and followers and gathers this support as a right due to his authority, support for the mystic is voluntarily given and does not arise from an organization. The mystic, because of his individualism, his lack of a church, and his nonparticipation in the economic system, cannot (and indeed does not wish to) take over the organization of a society; mysticism does not become the primary determinant of knowledge. It is reactionary, but it is not revolutionary.

Table 4 shows the structural differences between mysticism and religion by comparing the significant features of Calvinism, Mohammedanism, Buddhism, and Sūfism. It is clear that, while the first two are clearly similar in structure, the last two must be regarded as different phenomena.

---

[44] *Ibid.*, p. 209.

TABLE 4. A COMPARISON OF RELIGION AND MYSTICISM

	Religion		Mysticism	
	Calvinism	Mohammedanism	Buddhism	Sūfism
Type of thinking	rational-abstractive	rational-abstractive	empirical-abstractive	empirical-abstractive
Source of action	abstraction down from theoretic level	abstraction down from theoretic level	abstraction up from observational level	abstraction up from observational level
Conception of power source	supramundane god	supramundane god	Nirvana	extinction of self in merge with god
Nature of world	evil	transitory and empty	unknowable, to be accepted as observed and escaped from	unknowable, to be escaped from
Source of knowledge	revelation and authority through election—predestination	revelation and authority through election—predestination	example and practice	example and practice
Salvation			by individual action to eliminate dependence on the world	by individual action to eliminate dependence on the world

104

CHAPTER SEVEN

SCIENTIFIC DEVELOPMENT

To say that thinking which combines rationalism, empiricism, and abstraction is scientific, is not to make the empirical claim that this definition describes all thought which is typically regarded as scientific. "Science" ordinarily has ambiguous meanings depending upon the context in which it is used. Sometimes it is used to refer to fact gathering entirely lacking rationalistic application. The gathering of facts may be a preliminary step in scientific development as it is viewed here, but does not itself constitute science. Successful science may, on the other hand, appear empirically successful ("power" in a magical system of thought) if it is viewed only in terms of its results. While magical thinking pervades whole societies and religious thought divides social life into the sacred and the secular, it is clear that scientific thinking has a much smaller scope. Scientific thinking is more complex, and there has been no society in which science has predominated in determining thought. Sciences have instead formed subcultures separated by their distinctive mode of thought from the simple empiricism and/or rationalism in other sectors of societies.

Because of the nature of its structure, involving the interaction of empiricism, rationalism, and abstraction, scientific systems of knowledge are more subject to changes in content than are magical or religious systems. Therefore the examples will be considered historically. This chapter will concentrate on three quite different cases: (1) planetary astronomy, (2) classical mechanics, and (3) classificatory biology. The first and second cases are mathematical, the second is experimental, and the first and third utilize natural cases. Historically, astronomy has been closely associated with religion and mechanics with empiricism. Mechanics has often been viewed as the prototype of a systematic science; but biology is not usually so considered.

PLANETARY ASTRONOMY

Lacking the ability to survey retrospectively, we will never know with certainty what the average European of the Middle Ages thought about the cosmos. Educated classes did, however, record their views. The *Divine Comedy*, for example, was representative of the thought of this period.[1] Beginning with the Earth in the center and hell beneath its surface, Dante's universe consisted of nine concentric material spheres surrounded by a spiritual one.[2] The Earth was immobile while the nine material spheres moved around it. To the first sphere the moon was attached,[3] and its spots indicated its impure state.[4] The next sphere held Mercury,[5] then Venus,[6] followed by the Sun,[7] then Mars,[8] Jupiter,[9] and Saturn.[10] Beyond Saturn lay the sphere of the fixed stars,[11] and beyond that sphere was placed the last of the spheres, the *Primum Mobile*, so called since it was moved first and thus directed the motion of all others.[12] The last sphere represented the boundary of space and time, and beyond it lay heaven itself, at rest, the abode of God.

Dante peopled each sphere with souls, and he conceived of their motion as caused by spirits, apparently angels, "blessed movers."[13] The spheres were not merely paths and orbits of planets, sun, moon, and stars, but were actual material entities, although their material composition was not that of Earth. Dante shared the medieval view that Earth was composed of four elements: fire, air, water, and, as Butterfield puts it, "earth, which is the meanest stuff of all."[14] Each of these had its nature: earth and water had gravity, the tendency to fall when unsupported; and air and fire had the opposite quality, levity.[15] Above the earth, matter had an entirely different quality. The

---

[1] See Herbert Butterfield, *The Origins of Modern Science: 1300–1800* (New York: The Free Press, 1957), p. 29.

[2] See Dante Alighieri, *The Divine Comedy*, trans. by J.D. Sinclair (New York: Oxford University Press, 1948), III, 13.

[3] See *ibid.*, p. 33.

[4] See *ibid.*, pp. 39–41.

[5] See *ibid.*, p. 75.

[6] See *ibid.*, p. 117.

[7] See *ibid.*, p. 147.

[8] See *ibid.*, p. 201.

[9] See *ibid.*, p. 257.

[10] See *ibid.*, p. 303.

[11] See *ibid.*, p. 317.

[12] See *ibid.*, p. 398–99.

[13] *Ibid.*, p. 39.

[14] Butterfield, *Modern Science*, p. 30.

[15] See *ibid.*, p. 30.

crystalline spheres and the bodies they held were made up of a fifth element having neither the quality of gravity nor that of levity.

The nine spheres were viewed as wheeling about the Earth once each day pushed by their blessed movers, while the planets attached to them performed their own idiosyncratic fluctuations. The spheres apparently required pushing because (although the motion of all heavenly bodies was, as Plato decreed, circular[16]) they would slow down if not subject to the constant application of force.

The structure of Dante's universe was that of a hierarchy. Each of the elements was graded according to purity corresponding to its tendency to rise or fall (or, in the case of the fifth, according to its position in the cosmos). It was not only hierarchical in quality but in structure as well. Hell, basest of all, was most removed from God, while Earth was little better. Purity increased as one went out and up in the universe until perfection was reached in the tenth sphere, highest both physically and spiritually. To the believer, this system of the universe with God and all His angels looking down from on high at men at the bottom must have made a considerable impression. In it man's position combined the strategic advantage of the boy at the bottom of the well with the privacy of an ant fixed under a microscope.

From the point of view of modern astronomy, Dante's universe may seem insane, although rationally consistent in its madness. Dante, as "a true rationalist,"[17] was not very concerned with facts, and his universe was a theological system to him. Superficially, one might guess that even in Dante's time his conception of the cosmos must have been recognized as wholly metaphysical, a nice story and good for the faith but not relevant to the actual physical construction of the universe. Although such an inference is plausible, it is false. It was a metaphysical system to Dante, but it once had a scientific basis. Dante's work was so compelling precisely because it did correspond to the accepted conception of the physical universe, a conception based on the work of Ptolemy. Ptolemy's system of the universe was, in fact, a bad rational system; much better theories were proposed by other Greeks and were widely known in antiquity. In spite of its very real difficulties, it became the dominant view and retained its position through the Middle Ages when it was adapted to theological needs. Although it fit well the needs of Christian theology, it did not obtain its preeminence through the efforts of Christians but was used because of its scientific power.

Ptolemy's astronomy had its basis in Aristotle's conception of the universe. Aristotle's view, in turn, appears to have been influenced by two sources, Plato's authoritarian pronouncement on the necessity of circular motion of astronomical bodies and Eudoxus' mathematical theory as devel-

[16] See Arthur Koestler, *The Sleepwalkers: A History of Man's Changing Vision of the Universe* (New York: Grosset & Dunlap, 1963), p. 58.

[17] Butterfield, *Modern Science*, p. 31.

oped by Callippus.[18] As Ross points out, "Eudoxus had by an amazing mathematical feat succeeded in decomposing the apparent motion of the sun and moon into three rotatory movements."[19] These were mathematically conceived of as motions of constant velocity of one body, the sun, around a center which itself was in constant velocity around another center, itself in constant velocity around a third center, Earth. To the conception of the sun on its sphere rotating about the earth, Callippus found it necessary to add five spheres to explain the apparent motions of Mercury, Venus, and Mars. These motions were "apparent" in that they assumed the motionless Earth as a reference. According to Ross, the theory thus was a purely mathematical exercise.[20] But its character was completely changed by Aristotle.

Aristotle started with the argument that elements are simple bodies which "contain a principle of movement within themselves."[21] The simple motions of the four earthly elements are straight, two up and two down, while upward motion is contrary to downward motion. Suppose, Aristotle continued, that there is some other element; "if circular motion was contrary to its nature, it would have to have a natural simple motion contrary to the circular. But that is impossible."[22] Therefore, there is a fifth element whose motion is circular. Apparently the logical structure of this argument proved irresistible to the ancients.

Aristotle then pointed out that, of the simple figures, only the circle is perfect; thus the fifth element, since its natural motion is circular, must be more divine than the others.[23] But earthly bodies are subject to growth and decay since they are composed of elements whose natural motion is up or down. Circular motion, unlike a straight line, has neither beginning nor end, and consequently it is "ageless, unalterable, and impassive."[24] To the substance characterized by this perfect type of motion Aristotle gave the name *aither.*[25]

By similar arguments Aristotle established logically that both infinite bodies and a void are impossible. Thus the universe is bounded and full. Beyond this boundary there is "neither place nor void nor time."[26] This limit was termed "the first heaven."[27] On it were placed the fixed stars. "It

---

[18] See W.D. Ross, *Aristotle: A Complete Exposition of His Works & Thought* (New York: Meridian Books, 1959), p. 97.

[19] *Ibid.,* p. 97.

[20] See *ibid.,* p. 97.

[21] Aristotle, *On The Heavens,* trans. by W.K.C. Guthrie (Cambridge: Harvard University Press, 1939), p. 8.

[22] *Ibid.,* p. 9.

[23] See *ibid.,* pp. 9–10.

[24] *Ibid.,* p. 23.

[25] *Ibid.,* p. 25.

[26] *Ibid.,* p. 91.

[27] *Ibid.,* p. 146.

is a divine body, the proper activity of the divine is eternal life, which in a body must be manifested in the form of eternal motion, and the only motion which can be eternal is revolution in a circle."[28]

In view of this argument it is not very clear why the sun, moon, and planets do not have simple circular motion. But Aristotle explained this by their connection to actions on Earth. How could there be growth and decay of earthly objects which we all know to be influenced by the sun, moon, and planets if they had perfect circular motion?[29] Clearly they must not. Furthermore, the stars (being most removed from Earth) have the most perfect, most circular, motion whereas the motion of the other bodies is less so and is compounded of numbers of circular motions.[30] Aristotle's argument concluded with the observation that the Earth must be at rest since its natural motion is toward its own center and not around itself.[31]

Dante's view of the cosmos is clearly modeled on Aristotle's: the immobile Earth placed at the center of the universe; the circularity of motion of the stars and the circular wheels within wheels of the planets; the increasing purity of these bodies as their distance from the Earth increases; their composition from a fifth element; and their connection to invisible, but tangible, spheres. In fact, in a later observation in his *Metaphysics*, Aristotle extended his conception to include the notion that the cause of these circular motions is the action of spirits.[32] Aristotle conceived of God as the unmoved mover.[33] It is a small step to combine this notion with his idea of the cosmos, placing God just beyond the stars in the highest heaven of all. This place (being devoid of time and change) provides a fitting place for the Christian heaven and its eternal omnipotent God.

It must not be assumed that this theory of the cosmos was accepted by default merely because no one could think of a better alternative. On the contrary, to gain its preeminence this view had to compete with Herakleides' "Egyptian" system which (although geocentric) was simplified in that it conceived of Mercury and Venus as circling the sun. It also had to compete with the heliocentric system of Aristarchus who was, in Koestler's terms, the "last of the line of the Pythagorean astronomers."[34] Aristarchus' view was similar in its conception to Copernicus' in that it adhered to the dogma of circular movement; but he did place the sun in the center and the planets (including Earth) in motion about it. Although Aristarchus appears to have

[28] *Ibid.*, pp. 146–47.

[29] See *ibid.*, p. 148 *ff.*

[30] See *ibid.*, p. 202 *ff.*

[31] See *ibid.*, p. 240.

[32] See *ibid.*, pp. xxx-xxxi.

[33] See Aristotle, *Physics*, trans. by R. Hope (Lincoln: University of Nebraska Press, 1961), p. 178.

[34] Koestler, *Sleepwalkers*, p. 48.

done empirical work, apparently his system was not worked out (or at least not in detail) in connection with the available data.[35]

If Aristarchus' system was a better rational system than Aristotle's, it remains to be explained why the Aristotelian-Ptolemaic system predominated. Whewell maintained that, although the Greeks were able to effectively develop abstract ideas, "the next step in philosophizing, necessarily was to endeavor to make these vague abstractions more clear and fixed, so that the logical faculty should be able to employ them securely and coherently. But there were two ways of making this attempt; the one, by examining the words only, and the thoughts which they call up; the other, by attending to the facts and things which bring these abstract terms into use. The latter, the method of *real* inquiry, was the way to success; but the Greeks followed the former, the *verbal* or *notional* course, and failed."[36] In terms of the theory of scientific knowledge, Whewell's point is that there are two methods of inquiry utilizing abstraction: (1) *science*, which is connected to systematic empirical inquiry and thus is successful and (2) *theology*, which is not so connected and thus fails. The argument that the Greeks consistently utilized the latter type may be questioned. It is apparent that the Greeks did accept ideas that were not connected with empirical evidence; but, even under such circumstances, one might expect that theories which effectively connected empirical facts would be found more acceptable than those which did not.

From this point of view, in spite of the modern conception of the universe, Aristotle's theory of the cosmos was superior to Aristarchus' because it was directly based on the mathematical work of Eudoxus and Callippus describing the motions of the sun and planets. Aristotle's theory did have isomorphism with the facts then known. Since it was integrated with his physics, it offered a consistent rational system of considerable scope, much of which was connected isomorphically with the facts. In fact, the primary exponents of empirical methods in the seventeenth century were Aristotelians.[37]

In the second century, A.D., Ptolemy refined the rational system and established isomorphism between Aristotle's theory and the motions of the planets as they were then known.[38] Ptolemy's was the only astronomical theory of the time which was fully developed and in which the details of a consistent rational system fit the facts.[39] Certainly we recognize today that a heliocentric system is superior, but no heliocentric system was to be worked

---

[35] See *ibid.*, p. 49.

[36] William Whewell, *History of the Inductive Sciences* (London: John W. Parker and Son, 1857), p. 27.

[37] See Butterfield, *Modern Science*, Chap. 5.

[38] See Koestler, *Sleepwalkers*, p. 69.

[39] See Butterfield, *Modern Science*, p. 39.

out with Ptolemy's attention to detail until 1500 years later. Thus the potential of a heliocentric theory was not established, and, in its absence, the ancient and medieval world had a solid basis for accepting Ptolemy's system as scientifically superior. If Ptolemy's system was the only one with established isomorphism, then it might be expected to be maintained until one of superior isomorphism displaced it. Although other rational systems of superior logical integration and simplicity might be found, Ptolemy's system would be expected to be preserved as long as it was related to the facts and could be used for the calculation of the positions of sun, moon, planets, and stars.

Scientific power is dependent upon connection to the facts, not simplicity of rational structure. Ptolemy's theory was systematically related to the relevant facts. Others were not. Furthermore, the facts which were known did not contradict it. It is true that as the earth moves from one side of the sun to the opposite, the apparent positions of the stars change. This fact directly contradicts Ptolemy's system, but observation of it requires instruments of much greater accuracy than those then available. In fact, the only apparent motions to be explained were the daily and yearly motions of the sun, stars, and planets, and these were effectively explained. Because it fit the facts and was related in detail to them, Ptolemy's system had the greatest scientific power.

It has been maintained that modern astronomical thought began with Copernicus. The transformation of the center of the cosmos from Earth to the sun so fits the modern prejudice that Copernicus' work has been viewed as a major milestone in the history of thought. It is true that his rational system was better than Ptolemy's. Copernicus himself claimed to have reduced the total number of spheres necessary to explain the movements of heavenly bodies from Ptolemy's 80 to 34. (However, Koestler points out that the actual number Copernicus used was more than 50.)[40] Still, Copernicus' theory was rationally superior to Ptolemy's because of its comparative simplicity and resulting ease of calculation. With its 50 spheres, it was equally isomorphic with the facts when compared with Ptolemy's system, but it is clear that simplicity of calculation does not offer the decisive advantage of one system over another that isomorphism does. If two theories have equal isomorphism, the earlier one is expected to prevail in spite of greater ease of calculation of the later one. Acceptance of theory is related to scientific power, and in this case the power is equal, so the more familiar theory is likely to be retained. Ease of calculation, does not exhibit power in relation to familiarity. Thus in the United States we maintain an unwieldy, but familiar, system of measurement in terms of feet, yards, pounds, ounces, etc. when the metric system is available offering much greater ease of calcula-

[40] See Koestler, *Sleepwalkers*, p. 192.

tion. Ptolemy's system was maintained even though Copernicus' offered more simplicity merely because it was more familiar while both had equal scientific power.

The heliocentric view was not original to Copernicus but was a subject of speculation in antiquity and in the Middle Ages.[41] Copernicus' theory did not even offer new data, although data was then available of greater accuracy than that known in antiquity. Instead his system was supported exclusively by the data given by Ptolemy himself! Even more important is the fact that the Ptolemaic system had been rationalized by the middle of the fifteenth century by Peurbach, reducing the number of spheres from 80 to 40.[42] Thus, as Koestler explains, "contrary to popular, and even academic belief, Copernicus *did not reduce the number of circles, but increased them.*"[43] Therefore, it is no surprise that the heliocentric view had so little impact up until Kepler's time. *The Book of the Revolutions of the Heavenly Spheres,* Copernicus' major work, was a very poor seller for a work of such importance.[44] "Not even Galileo seems to have read it."[45] Nevertheless, Copernicus did offer the first alternative of equal power to the Ptolemaic system. Since it was not more powerful, it could not displace the Ptolemaic system, but, at the same time, it could not itself be rejected.

The Ptolemaic system was not only comparable in scientific power to Copernicus' theory and similar in ease of calculation after Peurbach's revision, but it also offered better scope. It was connected to Aristotle's mechanics, the only developed system of motion. Since Aristotle postulated that heavenly bodies were composed of *aither*, a fifth element, their physical properties could be viewed as different from those of earthly elements. In modern terms, this incorruptible matter was "subject to a different set of what we should call physical laws."[46] This not only separated earthly mechanics from that of the cosmos but made the idea of a motionless earth and a wheeling sky plausible.

Copernicus did not offer a new mechanics to explain the motions which he attributed to earth along with the moon and planets. In fact, from the point of view of the only theory of mechanics then in use, Copernicus' theory was implausible. He conceived of the weighty Earth as hurtling through the skies just as if it were made of *aither*. Its motion, being circular, was contrary to the nature of its elements to go either straight up or down. Putting oneself in the place of a sixteenth-century Aristotelian, the faults of

[41] See Butterfield, *Modern Science*, p. 39.
[42] See Koestler, *Sleepwalkers*, p. 192.
[43] *Ibid.*, p. 192. Butterfield, in fact, fell into exactly that error. See *Modern Science*, pp. 38–39.
[44] See Koestler, *Sleepwalkers*, p. 191.
[45] *Ibid.*, p. 192.
[46] Butterfield, *Modern Science*, p. 32.

the Copernican system are obvious. If it is accepted, the classical synthesis of mechanics and astronomy is broken down. It was not until Galileo's time that a system of mechanics was developed which made the Ptolemaic system appear unworkable. But this same system of mechanics with its concepts of inertia and acceleration made Copernicus' theory seem equally implausible. By the time Galileo's mechanical system was developed, however, Copernicus' theory was already passe.

There are times in the history of science when empiricism and rationalism seem to present themselves in their pure form in the thought of two people whose work, when synthesized, provides an important new scientific explanation. This was the case with Tycho and Kepler.

Tycho's importance was as an observer.[47] His own theory of the cosmos was a compromise in which the earth stood still while the planets circled the sun which, in turn, circled the earth. This theory was neither original nor in very exact agreement with his own observations. In fact, Tycho's only discovery, if it could be called that, was "that astronomy needed *precise* and *continuous* observational data."[48]

Nevertheless, it was precisely this new empirical development which affected the development of new ideas. In 1572 Tycho observed a new bright star. Such nova had been seen before but had been taken to be comets or shooting stars which, according to Aristotelian theory, were sublunar phenomena. Since all space beyond the moon was believed to be perfect and unchangeable, it was necessary to classify comets and shooting stars as sublunar phenomena in Aristotle's theory. But Tycho established the existence of a new star which did not move in relation to the others and thus must be classified as a new "fixed star" in contradiction to Aristotelian orthodoxy.

This was only the beginning of Tycho's observations. He accumulated great masses of data concerning the apparent motions of earth, moon, and planets with instruments of previously unparalleled accuracy.[49] But he would not publish the results of his observational work until he had developed a theory of his own and fit his observations to it. Kepler commented on Tycho's stubborn attitude that "Any single instrument of his cost more than my and my whole family's fortune put together. . . . My opinion of Tycho is this: he is superlatively rich, but he knows not how to make proper use of it as is the case with most rich people. Therefore, one must try to wrest his riches from him."[50] Kepler's notion of theory was scientific in that he did not believe it to consist of either a set of empirical facts or generalizations from

[47] See Koestler, *Sleepwalkers*, p. 335.
[48] *Ibid.*, p. 285.
[49] See *ibid.*, p. 288 *ff.*
[50] Quoted in *ibid.*, p. 278.

them. This is clear in his comment, "Tycho possesses the best observations, and thus so-to-speak the material for the building of the new edifice; he also has collaborators and everything he could wish for. He only lacks the architect who would put all this to use according to his own design."[51]

Kepler, in fact, recorded the stages of thought which brought him to the statement of the first and second laws of planetary motion. It was not a process of digesting Tycho's observational data and consequently generalizing "laws." Instead Kepler spent eight years considering the fit of one rational system after another in relation to the data until satisfactory isomorphism was established. In this process one after another of the Aristotelian hypotheses were thrown out. Kepler intended to present a new astronomical theory, but he realized that he must overthrow all of Aristotle's celestial mechanics in order to do so. Not only would the notion of spheres within spheres have to be eliminated, but the qualitative differentiation between celestial matter and Earthly matter would have to be displaced if the Earth were to be considered to be in motion. If his theory were to be successful, it would have to be fully integrated both conceptually and logically. In establishing his new theory he would not only have to point out the lack of isomorphism of the Ptolemaic-Aristotelian epicycles, but he would have to eliminate the logical basis for epicyclic constructions.

From Ptolemy's point of view the use of epicycles was merely a convenient tool "to save the appearances."[52] Its use supported the conception of the cosmos propounded by the authorities. Thus, for Kepler to eliminate the epicyclic approach to the computation of planetary orbits, it was also necessary to eliminate Aristotle's dogma. From a consideration of Copernicus' system, it became evident that Aristotle's physics could not be maintained with a heliocentric system. But Copernicus' wheels within wheels system had no physics compatible with it, nor was any ever developed. Kepler's task then entailed the development of an astronomical system along with a physics for it.

In Aristotle's system gravity was a tendency for earth and water to go down, while "down" was an absolute direction. Fire and air had the opposite direction to gravity, levity. Kepler attacked this as the central issue:

> It is therefore clear that the traditional doctrine about gravity is erroneous. ... Gravity is the mutual bodily tendency between cognate (i.e. material) bodies towards unity or contact (of which kind the magnetic force also is), so that the earth draws a stone much more than the stone draws the earth. ...
>
> Supposing that the earth were in the centre of the world, heavy bodies would be attracted to it, not because it is in the centre, but because it is a cognate (material) body. It follows that regardless where we place the earth ... heavy bodies will always seek it. ...

[51] Quoted in *ibid.*, p. 304.
[52] *Ibid.*, p. 73.

If two stones were placed anywhere in space near to each other, and outside the reach of force of a third cognate body, then they would come together, after the manner of magnetic bodies, at an intermediate point, each approaching the other in proportion to the other's mass (my italics).

If the earth and the moon where not kept in their respective orbits by a spiritual or some other equivalent force, the earth would ascend towards the moon one fifty-fourth part of the distance, and the moon would descend the remaining fifty-three parts of the interval, and thus they would unite. But the calculation presupposes that both bodies are of the same density.

If the earth ceased to attract the waters of the sea, the seas would rise and flow into the moon. . . .

If the attractive force of the moon reaches down to the earth, it follows that the attractive force of the earth, all the more, extends to the moon and even farther. . . .

Nothing made of earthly substance is absolutely light; but matter which is less dense, either by nature or through heat is relatively lighter. . . .

Out of the definition of lightness follows its motion; for one should not believe that when lifted up, it escapes to the periphery of the world, or that it is not attracted by the earth. It is merely less attracted than heavier matter, and is therefore displaced by heavier matter, so that it comes to rest and is kept in its place by the earth.[53]

This remarkable beginning seems only a step away from the Newtonian synthesis. Furthermore, Kepler started with a conception of the sun in the middle engaging in a tug of war with the planets circling it.[54] He thereby rejected the idea of uniform motion, assuming instead that the planets would be pushed faster as they approached the source of the force, the sun. Next he threw out the idea of perfect circles, substituting an egg-shaped figure. Soon thereafter he wrote to a friend that "if only the shape were a perfect ellipse all the answers could be found."[55] Only after some time did he see that Tycho's data fit the notion of an ellipse. After rationalizing the orbit of Mars, he fit the paths of other planets successfully into his conception of elliptical movement.

The isomorphism between the facts and the theory, the empirical and rational connections obtained when an elliptical figure was used, provided the scientific power for Kepler's first law. His second, that planets sweep out equal areas to their radii in equal times, also fit the facts. This isomorphism of a simpler, yet more logically developed, theory with more carefully collected data was sufficient to establish the scientific power of Kepler's work. In this case better isomorphism was established than that of the old Ptolemaic-Aristotelian theory (which, in fact, did not fit the new data) and this isomorphism was sufficient to displace the traditional view.

Kepler's theory was merely a beginning toward a new synthesis. He

[53] Quoted in *ibid.*, pp. 337–38.
[54] See *ibid.*, p. 316.
[55] *Ibid.*, p. 330.

had a clear notion of gravity as a force acting at a distance, but did not develop the conception of balanced forces of gravity and centripetal motion. Instead he put forward the idea of a whirlpool of *aither* generated by the sun which pushed the planets about their orbits. The closer they approached the sun, the more directly affected they were, so that their higher speed at apogee was explained.

The idea of a moving Earth now had to be accepted theoretically since Kepler's laws had the only satisfactory isomorphism with the new data, and the idea of a moving Earth meant that celestial and earthly mechanics were no longer separate studies.

Although there may be reason to suspect Aristotle of magical thinking, Ptolemy, Copernicus, Tycho, and Kepler did not believe that empirical connection was established by rules of thumb. None of them either engaged in empirical generalization or identified their constructed theories with the facts. Generality was obtained by the development of theoretic ideas which, in turn, were related to the facts by abstraction. Neither was their thinking theological: they were concerned with empirical connections. The theoretic component in their thought existed because of its isomorphism with the facts. It is true that Dante used Aristotle's theory theologically, but this does not prevent it from being used as a rational system in science.

The use of scientific knowledge in theology, as done in the Middle Ages, is a threat to the theology which, as religious knowledge, is supposed to be eternally true because it originates from the eternal omnipotent god-concept. But the basic character of scientific knowledge is dynamic. Scientific theories are subject to change, given new facts and new theories which fit them. As long as new facts were not obtained, the Ptolemaic system could not be displaced and theology was safe until new observations were made. If the theory has been incorporated into the theology, however, facts which contradict it are likely to shake the foundations of the theology. The basic character of the rational system can change rapidly in science, but this is impossible in religion. When theory is adjusted to fit the facts and the theology is not, they will come into conflict. Religions therefore have attempted to control science and suppress its development. This has been true not only of religions in the more conventional sense but also of political religions in totalitarian societies.

Scientific systems are not strictly empirical, and scientific revolutions are not political revolutions. A scientific revolution may occur if a strikingly different new theory replaces an established one. It does so because of its greater scientific power. Scientific revolutions are not the result of prevailing opinion or force of arms as are political revolutions, but rather simple demonstration of better isomorphism of a theory with the facts. Scientific knowledge is not magical and does not change with changes of empirical power. Perhaps the fact that new theories may be used to revolutionize magical systems is what has led some scholars (such as Thomas Kuhn in his book *The Structure of Scientific Revolutions*) to make this error.

Kuhn (following Karl Popper) also claims that theories are displaced by falsification; here again, he has confused magic with science. Theories are not displaced by new facts because they are not generalizations to be falsified by facts. One contrary fact does make a generalization false, but theory is not generalization and does not summarize facts. In this sense theories are not true or false, even when they do fit the facts, but are merely more or less powerful when used in explanation or prediction. As rational systems they can be replaced only by other rational systems and are typically displaced only by other theories of greater power. Tycho's new facts did not and could not by themselves result in the rejection of the Ptolemaic system. They were a threat to the theory because they were not isomorphic to it, but it took Kepler's theory to displace Ptolemy's.

Astronomical history occasionally points to man's irrationality, lack of perception, and stubbornness in sticking to a theory as bad as Ptolemy's for so long; but it would have been more irrational to reject Ptolemy's system while it fit the facts and no other theory fit them better.

MECHANICS

The Ptolemaic-Aristotelian system was the most powerful theory of antiquity. Comparatively speaking, Aristotle's mechanics was not even a theory for it is evident that isomorphism was never established between it and the phenomena to which it referred.

Aristotle's discussion of local motion logically begins with the definition of place: "A body is in a place if another body surrounds it."[56] This definition was directed toward his discussion of motion and void. It was the atomists' view that motion required void (space between the particles of matter), for if everything were packed solid, motion would be impossible. Aristotle's definition of place is offered in order to prove this notion false. Since motion of a body, according to Aristotle, is from place to place and place is defined as a body surrounded by another, and if void is the absence of a body, then logically motion in a void is impossible, or, in Aristotle's terms, "there would have to be complete stability ... neither would there be any place for anything to move to rather than to some other place."[57] Thus all motion is through a medium. Aristotle continued his attack on the notion of motion in a void by pointing out that there would be no reason "why anything set in motion would stop anywhere."[58] ... "Hence, a body

[56] Aristotle, *Physics*, p. 66.
[57] *Ibid.*, p. 71.
[58] *Ibid.*, p. 72. Of course, for Aristotle to make any statement at all, it was necessary for him to "cheat" on his previous definition of place and his earlier conclusion.

would either continue in its state of rest or would necessarily continue in its motion indefinitely, unless interfered with by a stronger force."[59] The latter was considered to be an obviously false statement—physically impossible. In spite of its obvious falsity to Aristotle, it bears a strong resemblance to Newton's first law: *"Every body continues in its state of rest, or of uniform motion in a right line, unless it is compelled to change that state by forces impressed upon it."*[60] This law was thus anticipated by Aristotle two thousand years before Newton formulated it; but it was presented as a false statement, devoid of meaning if related to his definition of place and also physically false.

Following his argument against the idea of motion in a void Aristotle concluded that "a body can continue moving only as long as it is propelled by something else."[61] In other words, it is motion itself, not acceleration, which must be explained and thus requires force for its maintenance. To explain motion, Aristotle divided motions into two types, *natural* and *violent.* Natural motions were natural tendencies of an object as a consequence of its composition. Those bodies composed of earth or water have gravity, the tendency to fall, whereas air and fire have levity, the tendency to rise. Violent motions result from the application of a force. Such motion continues only as long as the force continues and then quickly decays. This conception is, of course, consistent with his idea that motion is always through a body, for Aristotle fully understood that bodies offer resistance to motion. This conception is likewise consistent with observation: as long as a wagon is pulled, it will continue in motion, but it will soon come to rest if the pulling is stopped. For some observed motions Aristotle's idea of motion reflects day-to-day experience more closely than that entailed in Newtonian mechanics.

Nevertheless, some types of motion, particularly projectile motion, cannot be easily placed in this scheme. Projectile motion requires a special explanation, for it continues for some time after the application of force has stopped. Thus an arrow ought to fall to the ground immediately after leaving the bow string. Aristotle offered the following argument: "the air which has been pushed pushes projectiles with a motion more vigorous than their motion in their resident place."[62] But he contended that this could not happen in a void, for "a body can continue moving only as long as it is propelled by something else."[63] In other words, projectiles continue because they are blown along by a wind created in their critical push. Aristotle's idea of motion has its problems if it is applied to projectile motion.

---

[59] Ibid., p. 72.

[60] Isaac Newton, "Planetary Motion and the System of the World," *Studies in Explanation,* ed. by Russell Kahl (Englewood Cliffs: Prentice-Hall, 1963), p. 71.

[61] Aristotle, *Physics,* p. 72.

[62] *Ibid.,* p. 72.

[63] *Ibid.,* p. 72.

It might seem that celestial motions would be inconsistent with this idea of motion; but Aristotle avoided this problem because heavenly bodies were described as being made up of a fifth element whose physical properties were entirely different. Their motion did not enter into the discussion of local motion at all.

Aristotle likewise had difficulties in his conception of different velocities. In natural motion, different speeds were attributed to either differences in the medium through which the matter traversed or differences in the weight of the body.[64] (Of course, with his idea of absolute up and down and qualitative levity and gravity, Aristotle did not distinguish mass from weight.) Quantitatively, in terms of the medium, Aristotle stated that the time required for motion is "in proportion to the density of the hindering body."[65] In other words, in a medium twice as dense, a body of a given weight would fall half as fast; in a medium ten times as dense it would fall one-tenth as fast; and so forth. From this ratio, he further concluded that, since the density of a void is zero, velocity through it would be instantaneous![66] Aristotle postulated that "heavy and light bodies move with unequal velocities over an equal space in the ratio which their magnitudes have to each other."[67] As long as motion is limited to motion through a medium, then, the first part of the statement appears true—if two bodies have the same density, the heavier will fall faster because the areas of the bodies (which determine their resistance to the medium) increase only to the square of their linear dimensions while their mass (which determines the force pushing them through the medium) increases to the cube of their linear dimensions. But the factor is more complex than a simple proportion of weights and is considerably less in air than he assumed. Furthermore, it is only relevant to the terminal speeds. Until their maximum speed is approached, all bodies will accelerate in air at about the same rate. Thus, if the fall were short enough that terminal velocities were not reached, the data would not confirm Aristotle's view. Only if the fall were long enough would the proportionately greater speed of the more massive object result in a shorter period of fall. It is consequently no surprise that at Galileo's time the Aristotelians argued for higher places from which to drop bodies while Galileo preferred to drop them from lower places where uniform acceleration would be more evident.

Empirically, Aristotle's error in proportion of speeds through air is less significant than it might seem. In the absence of ideal conditions, experiments do not fit theories exactly, so the goodness of fit (or lack of fit) would

[64] See *ibid.*, p. 72.
[65] *Ibid.*, p. 72.
[66] See *ibid.*, p. 73.
[67] *Ibid.*, p. 74.

not immediately lead to the rejection of a theory. In fact, the idea that heavy things fall faster seems to have been generally considered more important than their precise proportional speed. If the quantitative elements of Aristotle's system are ignored, the qualitative picture appears to fit fairly well some of the normal day to day motions we see around us. But quantitatively the system has grave defects which, unlike those of his view of the cosmos, could not be hidden by complicated epicycles. Furthermore, although rejection of his cosmic theory ultimately required more exact data which was both mathematically difficult and expensive to obtain, almost anyone with a minimum of education could have established that the speed of motion was not inversely proportional to the density of the medium or directly proportional to the weight of the object. With the possible exception of a small quantitative portion and a few assumptions relevant to it, the rest of his mechanics was not scientific theory at all. The other parts simply were not relevant to empirical connections, but were theoretic and had the logical character of theology. As such, they fit in easily with developing Christianity. Aristotle, for example, discussed motion in terms of causes. For each motion he conceived a prior motion (or mover) which caused it and which, in turn, had its own mover, and so on until the prime mover is reached (the power-concept) which Aristotle called God. The same argument was used later by Aquinas as one proof of the existence of God.

The portions of Aristotle's mechanical system which were related to empirical observations were not connected with the sort of careful observation which characterized the Ptolemaic system. Careful observation alone would have made it obvious that the simple proportions between speed, density, and weight could not be maintained. In that sense, even these parts of the system were more theological than scientific. Aristotle's mechanics, however, enjoyed the status of a theory and was not displaced by the facts alone but only by Galileo's more powerful theoretic system.

Galileo began his discussion of falling bodies with a rejection of Aristotle at two levels, observational and theoretic. On the observational level, he commented that "I greatly doubt that Aristotle ever tested by experiment whether it be true that two stones, one weighing ten times as much as the other, if allowed to fall, at the same instant, from a height of, say, 100 cubits, would so differ in speed that when the heavier had reached the ground, the other would not have fallen more than 10 cubits."[68] He added that he had performed the experiment himself and found "that a cannon ball weighing one or two hundred pounds, or even more, will not reach the ground by as much as a span ahead of a musket ball weighing only half a pound, provided both are dropped from a height of 200 cubits."[69]

---

[68] Galileo, "On Falling Bodies," *Studies in Explanation*, ed. by Kahl, p. 34.
[69] *Ibid.*, p. 34.

On the theoretic level Galileo argued that, given two bodies whose natural speeds are different (according to their different weights, as Aristotle believed), if they are attached to one another, the more rapid one will pull the slower while the slower will retard the more rapid.[70] As a result, the compound body should have a natural speed somewhere between the two.[71] But, since the compound body is heavier than either of the bodies which made it up, this conclusion violates the idea that heavier bodies fall faster, demonstrating logically that Aristotle's rational structure was internally contradictory. From the empirical facts given and the rational argument, Galileo inferred "that large and small bodies move with the same speed provided they are of the same specific gravity."[72]

Having rejected the first of Aristotle's ideas of falling bodies, Galileo considered the idea of a void. Since he was unable to create a vacuum, he used liquids and gasses of less and less density to gain successive approximations of that state. The idea of a void began to take on the character of an ideal condition, a theoretic concept, for his theory. He observed that, as the density of the medium reduces, the rates of fall of lighter and heavier objects get closer and closer. "Having observed this I came to the conclusion that in a medium totally devoid of resistance all bodies would fall with the same speed."[73] Through further experimentation, now with inclined planes which he used to reduce the effect of air resistance,[74] he reported that "during equal intervals of time [a falling object] receives equal increments of momentum and velocity."[75]

It is evident that Galileo's procedure did not rely exclusively on the use of empirical facts to reject the "superstitions" of Aristotle but involved instead a careful choice of facts to investigate in light of his alternative theory. All of the empirical work which he did was a consequence of his theoretical ideas. His experiments were not random like those of the alchemists, but were a consequence of his theory which, in turn, was developed to be iso-morphic to the facts as they were established.

For his rational system Galileo employed the principles of geometry and consequently, following Descartes, thought of natural motion as a straight line and of mass as a concentrated point (although the full elabora-tion of these ideas did not take place until Newton). Furthermore, his idea of natural motion was the opposite of Aristotle's and depended on the con-ception of a vacuum as an ideal condition. He was not therefore only interested in dropping objects from very high places but in fact preferred

---

[70] See *ibid.*, p. 34.
[71] See *ibid.*, p. 35.
[72] *Ibid.*, p. 35.
[73] *Ibid.*, p. 39.
[74] See *ibid.*, p. 43.
[75] *Ibid.*, p. 40.

to roll balls down inclined planes where observation was easier and, more importantly, where the ideal empirical circumstances implied by his developing rational system were more closely approximated.[76]

Galileo himself fully realized the dependence of the choice of facts on the theory, for he noted that "the principles, once established by well-chosen experiments, become the foundation of the entire superstructure."[77]

His next consideration was the motion of projectiles. Here he began by assuming a lack of air resistance so that he could assume a uniform horizontal motion. Motion, then, could be understood as a compound of horizontal and uniformly accelerated vertical motion.[78] From these assumptions he proceeded directly with the mathematical proof that the curve so described must be a parabola.[79] Only then did he consider the fit of these notions with the facts. Here again, we see the development of science through the interplay of rational ideas and empirical facts.

Nevertheless, in contrast to Galileo, it should be noted that all work which calls itself scientific is not necessarily so, simply because it utilizes manipulation. Behavioral experiments are a good example. Consider the meaning of the following comments.

> The experiment is performed for other reasons than to test the adequacy of the hypothesis. Nor will the outcome of the experiment be judged a success or failure in terms of its agreement or disagreement with the prediction. This point emphasizes an important property of experiments that are designed to answer the "I wonder what will happen if . . . " type of question. Such experiments, if they meet adequate criteria of reliability and generality, *never produce negative results*. Data can be negative only in terms of a prediction. When one simply asks a question of nature, the answer is always positive. Even an experimental manipulation that produces no change in the dependent variable can provide useful and often important information. . . . All the significant data have not yet turned up in the laboratory.[80] . . . Intensive cultivation of an area of research by an alert observer will inevitably bring out interrelations among the phenomena comprising that area. The interrelations will take the form of similarities among the variables that are relevant to the different phenomena.[81]

The method advocated here is empirical and will lead to magical knowledge. The idea is to go into the lab and manipulate observables in order to establish their relation to other observables. The statement of results, when it is general, is in terms of the connection of the class of objects

[76] See Butterfield, *Modern Science*, Chap. 11.

[77] Galileo, "Naturally Accelerated and Projectile Motion," *Studies in Explanation*, ed. by Kahl, p. 57.

[78] See *ibid.*, p. 60.

[79] See *ibid.*, p. 61.

[80] Murray Sidman, *Tactics of Scientific Research* (New York: Basic Books, 1960), pp. 8–9.

[81] *Ibid.*, p. 15.

manipulated to the class of objects supposedly affected, and is therefore an empirical generalization. The judgment of connection is concerned with the deviation of effects from chance expectation and usually uses a test of statistical significance. The judgment of connection has nothing to do with isomorphism but is instead completely empirical.

The empirical generalizations which result from these experiments are tendency statements, not theoretic laws, and thus are not useful for scientific explanation. These empirical generalizations are isolated from one another because their empirical character does not allow them to be connected in a rational scheme. Although this information may have immediate practical or technical value, it does not have theoretic value or explanatory use. It certainly has nothing to do with science, and those sociologists and psychologists who use it have not contributed to scientific knowledge.

Galileo's conception of the experiment was entirely different. For him an experiment was rationally guided, and empirical relations were not judged by tests of significance. No statistics were used or needed. The test of an empirical connection was its isomorphism to his theory, while the test of his theory was its isomorphism with his empirical observations. Interdependence through abstraction was the means, and the end reached was a powerful theory. If Galileo had used the experimental method of contemporary psychology and sociology, his results would have been completely different. If he had followed a strategy of "I wonder what would happen if . . . " he would have taken a sample of objects representative of those common in his time: cannon balls, bricks, slates, pieces of paper, feathers, wood, and so forth, and proceeded to drop them from varying heights. The result would have been a different set of facts from those he concerned himself with. If modern statistical techniques had been available, he could have used them as a means of establishing a set of empirical connections. Using Aristotle's theory to determine expected frequencies, he could show with a chi square test that in most cases the data was significantly different from that expected. He could have correlated height and time taken to fall, and accounted for much of the second in terms of the first for any single object. Comparing objects at one height, he could have accounted for somewhat more than half the variance by their weight alone. No scientific advancement would be gained by this because it has no theoretic component, no explanatory power. It would be simple description and would not have had the power to overthrow Aristotle's theory.

Galileo presented himself to his contemporaries as orthodox in his religious beliefs. In spite of this, he had a serious disagreement with the Church. This might have been expected because the theoretical component of his work directly contradicted established theology. From the religious point of view, theology was the "queen of the sciences." Any theory which contradicted theology was claimed by the orthodox Church Fathers to be false. Galileo presented an alternative view.

> I hear them pretend to the power of constraining others by scriptural authority to follow in a physical dispute that opinion which they think best agrees with the Bible, and then believe themselves not bound to answer the opposing reasons and experiences. In explanation and support of this opinion they say that since theology is queen of all the sciences, she need not bend in any way to accommodate herself to the teachings of less worthy sciences which are subordinate to her; these others must rather be referred to her as to their supreme empress, changing and altering their conclusions according to her statutes and decrees. . . . I question whether there is not some equivocation in failing to specify the virtues which entitle sacred theology to the title of "queen." . . . Hence it seems likely that regal pre-eminence is given to theology in the second sense; that is, by reason of its subject and the miraculous communication of divine revelation of conclusions which could not be conceived by men in any other way, concerning chiefly the attainment of eternal blessedness. . . . her professors should not arrogate to themselves the authority to decide on controversies in professions which they have neither studied nor practiced. . . . I entreat those wise and prudent Fathers to consider with great care the difference that exists between doctrines subject to proof and those subject to opinion. Considering the force exerted by logical deductions, they may ascertain that it is not in the power of the professors of demonstrative sciences to change their opinions at will and apply themselves first to one side and then to the other.[82]

Galileo, in fact, supported science rather than religion, as a basis of knowledge in those areas in which they were in contradiction. Since Galileo lived in the midst of a religious system, his efforts were unsuccessful. But in the long run theology has retreated before scientific theory, and religion, in defense, has attempted to interpret theory as less sure than the revealed truth of theology. Monkey trials seem successful at the outset when religion is more prevalent than science, but they lose ground in the long run. A revolution in scientific thinking occurs each time a new, more powerful, theory is introduced, but a revolution in general thought takes much longer.

Galileo and Kepler separately displaced two of Aristotle's theories; but the work of these two men had not been rationalized. Both Kepler's mechanics and Galileo's view of the cosmos had their problems. The synthesizing idea was that of universal gravity proposed by Newton.[83] It is not necessary to enter into the details of that theory or the facts to which it has been connected, for it is evident that it is a rationalistic theory isomorphic

---

[82] Galileo, *Discoveries and Opinions of Galileo*, trans. by S. Drake (Garden City: Doubleday & Company, 1957), pp. 191–94.

[83] Newton, unlike Kepler and Galileo, worked together with a group of other scientists in developing his ideas. The circle included Halley, Wren, and Hooke. See Koestler, *Sleepwalkers*, p. 502.

to a set of facts.[84] It is also evident from direct reference in his own work that Newton's system of the world is a synthesis of the ideas of Kepler and Galileo. But it is significant that Newton's work has that character in spite of his obvious empiricist leanings.

From a contemporary point of view, Newton's idea of gravity is a rational concept only. It is the means by which the synthesis was obtained. Today it is not necessary to think of it as a material force. With the *idea* of gravity, calculations could be made which were established as isomorphic to motions of objects from place to place. But these calculations required that one conceive of action performed at a distance. Nevertheless to Newton, as to Hume, force required the contact of bodies. Newton stated that "It is inconceivable that inanimate brute matter should, without the mediation of something else, which is not material, operate upon, and affect other matter without mutual contact."[85] Thus Newton in his private thoughts took a Humian billiard ball notion of the universe, a universe like Aristotle's which had to be filled up. So, like Aristotle, Newton conceived of motion as absolute through ether. To Newton innate gravity was an absurdity which "no man who has in philosophical matters a competent faculty of thinking, can ever fall into."[86] Not matter, but an agent, is the cause of motion, and in that sense Newton would put Aristotle's spirits back in the universe. Kepler's and Galileo's scientific thought was more elegant.

Although a product of true British empiricism, Newtonian mechanics is a theoretic system. It consists of a rational system linked by abstraction to sets of observations of individual empirical facts. These facts are connected through isomorphism to the theory. Newton's theory displaced Galileo's and Kepler's because of greater power in its broader scope and better isomorphism.

BIOLOGICAL EVOLUTION

Scientific theories, however, do not have to be mathematical, nor do they have to have quantitative referents. Charles Darwin's theory of evolution is a case of this type. Before Darwin's theory, the most significant notion of organic evolution was that of Jean Baptiste Lamarck who conceived of a mechanical evolution of animals to higher forms determined by a "law of progress." Like man, according to Lamarck, individual animals developed through accumulated experiences and habits which were inherited by their offspring and thus led progressively to higher forms.[87]

[84] See Newton, "Planetary Motion," and Butterfield, *Modern Science*, Chap. 8.
[85] Quoted in Koestler, *Sleepwalkers*, p. 503.
[86] Quoted in *ibid.*, p. 503.
[87] See Stephen F. Mason, *A History of the Sciences* (New York: Collier Books, 1962), pp. 326–29.

Darwin's grandfather, Erasmus Darwin, added to this notion that animals have an innate ability to improve themselves—an idea of evolution through the survival of the more healthy forms in competition.[88] In fact, the notion of evolution existed for some time in human thought, but it was a conception of linear evolution which did not fit the empirical classifications of animals and thus had no relevance to either classification or explanation of the variety of species.

Linnaeus, a Swedish contemporary of Lamarck and Erasmus Darwin, developed a means of classifying animals and plants by giving each a generic name relating to a group of similar animals and plants and a species name indicating the particular kind.[89] Lamarck attempted to set up a classificatory system like that of Linnaeus which could be related to a theory of linear evolution. But the empirical facts did not fit the theory, and his straight line classification began to look more like the modern genealogical tree.[90] Lamarck's linear evolutionary theory could not be made isomorphic to his classifications. Thus, although there were classificatory and evolutionary theories prior to Darwin, isomorphism was not established.

Charles Darwin's theory of evolution began with his recognition of the inadequacy of previous theories, continued through a careful study of the available empirical data on plants and animals, and culminated in an integration of other's ideas in a theory of evolution. He wrote:

> I worked on true Baconian principles, and without any theory collected facts on a wholesale scale, more especially with respect to domesticated productions, by printed inquiries, by conversation with skilful breeders and gardeners, and by extensive reading ... I soon perceived that selection was the keystone of man's success in making useful races of animals and plants. But how selection could be applied to organisms living in a state of nature remained for some time a mystery to me.[91]

Darwin's use of "Baconian principles" did point out to him the significant fact that animals and plants could be selectively bred for desired characteristics. This observation contradicted previous notions of innate intent in biological evolution, but it did not explain the mechanism. He was unable to draw a theory out of his data.

But Malthus' notion that men reproduce geometrically while their food supply increases arithmetically, later provided the inspiration for his theory:

> In October 1838, that is fifteen months after I had begun my systematic

---

[88] See *ibid.*, pp. 329–30.
[89] See Clarence J. Goodnight and Marie L. Goodnight, *Zoology* (St. Louis: C.V. Mosby Company, 1954), p. 42.
[90] See Mason, *Sciences*, p. 345.
[91] Quoted in *ibid.*, pp. 415–16.

enquiry, I happened to read for amusement Malthus on Population, and being well prepared to appreciate the struggle for existence which everywhere goes on from long continued observation of the habits of animals and plants, it at once struck me that under these circumstances favourable variations would tend to be preserved, and unfavourable ones to be destroyed. The result of this would be the formation of a new species. Here then I had at last got a theory by which to work.[92]

Darwin's theory incorporated the notions of several social and biological thinkers, including: (1) from Malthus the idea of competition for existence, (2) from Spencer the notion of survival of the fittest, (3) from Lamarck the idea of inherited characteristics, (4) and the idea of evolution. Each of these conceptions was revised in the context of Darwin's theory.

When Darwin formulated his theory, genetic laws were unknown. The Mendelian laws were not to be established for another 20 years. But he observed that man was able to select animals for certain desired characteristics and breed them for an improved stock:

We cannot suppose that all the breeds were suddenly produced as perfect and as useful as we now see them; indeed, in many cases, we know that this has not been their history. The key is man's power of accumulative selection: nature gives successive variations; man adds them up in certain directions useful to him. In this sense he may be said to have made for himself useful breeds.[93]

But this did not explain differences among natural species. These, according to Darwin, were based on "natural selection" which worked by the mechanism of competition for survival and resulting selection of favorable characteristics. It may likewise be observed that individuals of a species vary:

The many slight differences which appear in the offspring from the same parents, or which it may be presumed have thus arisen, from being observed in the individuals of the same species inhabiting the same confined locality, may be called individual differences. No one supposes that all the individuals of the same species are cast in the same actual mould. These individual differences are of the highest importance for us, for they are often inherited, as must be familiar to every one; and they thus afford materials for natural selection to act on and accumulate, in the same manner as man accumulates in any given direction individual differences in his domesticated productions.[94]

Differences in species thus result from the accumulated selection of different characteristics favorable to existence in the struggle for life.

Owing to this struggle, variations, however slight and from whatever cause proceeding, if they be in any degree profitable to the individuals of a species,

---

[92] Quoted in *ibid.*, p. 416.
[93] Charles Darwin, *The Origin of Species* (New York: Mentor Books, 1958), p. 48.
[94] *Ibid.*, p. 59.

in their infinitely complex relations to other organic beings and to their physical conditions of life, will tend to the preservation of such individuals, and will generally be inherited by the offspring. The offspring, also, will thus have a better chance of surviving, for, of the many individuals of any species which are periodically born, but a small number can survive. I have called this principle, by which each slight variation, if useful, is preserved, by the term Natural Selection, in order to mark its relation to man's power of selection.[95]

The struggle for existence is, in turn, based on the limited capacity of the natural environment to support its creatures:

A struggle for existence inevitably follows from the high rate at which all organic beings increase. Every being, which during its natural lifetime produces several eggs or seeds, must suffer destruction during some period of its life, and during some season or occasional year, otherwise, on the principle of geometric increase, its numbers would quickly become so inordinately great that no country could support the product. Hence, as more individuals are produced than can possibly survive, there must in every case be a struggle for existence, either one indivudal with another of the same species, or with the individuals of distinct species, or with the physical conditions of life. It is the doctrine of Malthus applied with manifold force to the whole animal and vegetable kingdoms; for in this case there can be no artificial increase of food, and no prudential restraint from marriage. Although some species may now be increasing, more or less rapidly, in numbers, all cannot do so, for the world would not hold them.[96]

Darwin's notion of evolution is not linear. It suggests that each genus will be represented by a diversification of species based on the selection of physical characteristics favorable to survival under diverse conditions. It is consequently isomorphic to the tree-like classification structure which results from the attempt to organize plants and animals according to their observed natural differences. Darwin wrote:

The affinities of all the beings of the same class have sometimes been represented by a great tree. I believe this simile largely speaks the truth. The green and budding twigs may represent existing species; and those produced during former years may represent the long succession of extinct species. At each period of growth all the growing twigs have tried to branch out on all sides, and to overtop and kill the surrounding twigs and branches, in the same manner as species and groups of species have at all times overmastered other species in the great battle for life. The limbs divided into great branches, and these into lesser and lesser branches, were themselves once, when the tree was young, budding twigs, and this connection of the former and present buds by ramifying branches may well represent the classification of all extinct and living species in groups subordinate to other groups.[97]

[95] *Ibid.*, p. 74.
[96] *Ibid.*, p. 75.
[97] *Ibid.*, pp. 129–30.

Darwin's evolutionary theory is not mathematical, but it is nevertheless an explanatory theory of integrated concepts which is isomorphic to the existing data. It has the characteristic of nonlimited scope in that it applies to all plants and animals in their natural surroundings in which there is a limited supply of resources. Its universality is not a result of generalization, but of theoretical construction.

The theory may be summarized as follows:

1. Given the reproduction of animals (and plants) and limited environmental resources, we can expect

2. competition for survival, which

3. when individuals vary in their physical characteristics, will lead to

4. the survival of those who have physical characteristics which best enable them to make use of the resources, and therefore

5. interbreeding of the survivors with such naturally selected characteristics, followed by

6. modification into various species after several generations, which, in turn,

7. modifies the environment, and thus the process is cumulative.

Although this theory is not mathematical, it is integrated, predictive, and isomorphic with the facts. It has been instrumental to the development of biology. Darwin himself predicted several changes in the biological sciences that should follow his theory. It is perhaps not remarkable that he anticipated changes, but it is clearly significant that these particular changes actually took place. As he expected, biological classification became a genealogy of the species. Also:

> A grand and almost untrodden field of inquiry will be opened, on the causes and laws of variation, on correlation, on the effects of use and disuse. ... Species and groups of species which are called aberrant, and which may fancifully be called living fossils, will aid us in forming a picture of the ancient forms of life. Embryology will often reveal to us the structure, in some degree obscured, of the prototype of each great class.[98]

Darwin's theory made explanation possible, and the existence of a rational explanation made it possible to predict changes through rational extension.

SCIENCE AND SOCIAL STRUCTURE

Theory, in the long run, has displaced theology when they have been in contradiction, but this has occurred primarily in societies which were politically empirical in orientation. In societies which have a political

---

[98] *Ibid.*, p. 448.

theology, such as Communist Russia and Nazi Germany, the result has been different. In these cases theories have been suppressed if they conflicted with the prevailing theology. Most modern development under these conditions has been technological rather than scientific. Mason points out that under Nazi rule there was a

> decline in the number of students reading scientific subjects in the German universities. The decline was most marked in theoretical physics. . . . Empiricism was favoured in German science under the Third Reich because it agreed with the glorification of the man of action, and because the theories of science tended to contradict the tenets of national-socialism. . . . The most important single historical consequence was a decline of fundamental research.[99]

In technological areas, such as aircraft design and manufacture, the Nazis were successful; but in other areas, such as atomic research and radar, which were dependent upon scientific development, they were not competitive. The influence of political religion on science is well illustrated in that case. Science is eliminated in favor of empiricism which poses no threat to the authoritarian system of knowledge and is immediately useful.

The relationship between political empiricism and science is different. Physical science poses no threat to political empiricism by its use of theoretic connection and, if controlled, it can be useful. Much of the development of scientific knowledge has been in societies dominated by political empiricism. Individuals holding empirical power in magical systems of knowledge may choose whether or not to support particular kinds of scientific research, and the scientific work that is done is done under conditions determined by the empirically powerful. Even Archimedes, whose laws of levers and "principle" are remembered today, made his living as an architect and military engineer to the Tyrant of Syracuse. Since that time, national states have attempted to control science for their own empirical ends with varying degrees of success. The development of science has, in fact, been somewhat related to its support by empirical power. The developments of astronomy, ballistics, and atomic reasearch have been provided with support and have, in turn, supported the empirical power structure.

The results of this subordination of science to empirical power have been frequently noted, and science has been blamed for them. But such criticisms of science as C. Wright Mills' attack on it for its "technological climax in the H-bomb" and his comment that "Many cultural workmen have come to feel that science is a false and pretentious Messiah"[100] have misdirected their attack. Mills and his followers have failed to see that what they are really attacking is technology in an empirically dominated system

---

[99] Mason, *Sciences*, p. 586.
[100] C. Wright Mills, *The Sociological Imagination* (New York: The Oxford University Press, 1959), pp. 15–16.

and not science at all. Science is not working for its own goals but is subordinated to empirical goals of worldly power.

One of the faults inherent in Mills' critique is the judgment of science in terms of his experience in sociology. Sociology, however, is not now a science. It has no theories isomorphic with any empirical facts, and it offers no scientific explanations. Given scientific development, so-called "social problems" could be solved. But sociology has adopted the empirical methods of educational psychology and has become almost purely magical in its form. This condition prevails throughout the social sciences.

The lopsided development of science in favor of physical, chemical, and biological science over the social sciences is not due to the complexity of data of the social sciences or any of the other excuses that are bandied about—all data is complex until subsumed under a rational system of explanation. Robert K. Merton has argued that this is a consequence of the differing extent of effort and time spent, but this idea is clearly false. The effort put into studying society has been much greater up to this time than the total effort in the physical sciences up to Galileo's time. Yet social science has not developed even that far. Magical empirical power, whether political or economic, has thus been able to control most scientific work in Western societies. If social science were to develop scientifically, it is probable that its scientific power would replace the present magical power in these societies and the whole basis of the present power structures. It is doubtful, however, that this development would be popular in the present power circles; the economic and political structures, as long as they are based on magical power, will continue to reserve support for physical sciences and for empirical work only in the social sciences. Social science, if it develops, will have to develop on its own.

Science cannot attack a magical system of knowledge directly because science does not rely on empirical power; on the other hand, magical knowledge cannot be maintained against scientific knowledge. Radical change in social conditions must clearly be preceded by the development of social science.

Although the development of science has been supported by magical power when it will facilitate the reaching of empirical goals, it requires rationalism in order to exist. Like religion, science requires a separation of mental and manual labor in order to provide the conditions in which theoretic connection can be made. Science, however, involves the reintegration of mental and manual labor when connection at the theoretic level is abstracted to the observational level. Science began its development in Greece in the work of some individuals, such as Aristotle and Archimedes, who combined a background of manual labor with mental training (or vice versa) while they were still separated in the society as a whole.

In spite of their great effect on magical society, those who hold and have held science as a basis of knowledge are few in numbers. Their work is used by great numbers of technologists and engineers for empirical uses, but scientific knowledge has never taken over a society. It might be possible to attribute this to its existence and exploitation by empirical power-holders in a magical society and the attempt to suppress scientific power; however, it is more likely that the very complexity of the thinking required to utilize a scientific knowledge system puts it at a disadvantage when compared with other systems. It requires skill in three types of thinking, empirical, rational, and abstractive, and more mental and observational training is needed to utilize it. Few societies are equipped to train the majority of the people in these skills.

CHAPTER EIGHT

THE PROBLEM OF KNOWLEDGE IN THE MODERN WORLD

The problem of knowledge in the modern world is concerned with the relation of knowledge systems to one another and to existing forms of social organization. Individual subcultures include magic, religion, mysticism, and science. In the more developed nations improvements in communication have brought these systems of knowledge into close contact, decisively affecting the conditions of life today.

In Western nations the development of science has had a significant influence on religious knowledge. The medieval synthesis of knowledge organized under Catholicism was first brought into question by Kepler and Galileo, and the scientific development of their ideas by Newton segregated science and religion by limiting the area to which religious knowledge could be applied. The conflict generated by this process of scientific development continued through the nineteenth century supported by the rise of Darwinian theory. Weber pointed out that one effect of the progressive limitation of scope of religious knowledge was that religion, once a source of rationalism, was pushed into an ever more irrational position.[1] Protestantism has consequently been separated into sect and church. Sects have remained religious in their type of knowledge and have gathered their members from the ranks of the powerless; but they are able to maintain their system of knowledge only through isolation from society as a whole, and this, along with a lack of actual participation in the educational structure, leaves the individual mem-

[1] See Max Weber, *From Max Weber: Essays in Sociology*, trans. and ed. by H.H. Gerth and C. Wright Mills (New York: Oxford University Press, 1958), p. 281.

bers ignorant of other systems of knowledge. Churches, on the other hand, draw their members from the more powerful and more highly educated and have consequently been less concerned with religion and more with social gospel which includes a magical orientation. Catholicism too has been increasingly divided by power and scientific development to an extent perhaps never equalled since the Council of Nicaea. The consequence of all this is that the importance of religion as a system of knowledge has declined.

The central problems of modern civilization, the destructive potential of modern warfare, the threat to survival as a consequence of environmental pollution, the institutionalization of poverty and racism, the concentration of power and the associated suppression of dissent, have resulted in a remarkable increase in mysticism which previously had little impact on Western civilization. Mysticism offers escape, either with or without the use of drugs—an escape which attenuated religion is less able to provide. But the escape of the mystic is individual and cannot solve the problems from which he removes himself. The source of these problems and their solution, the very survival of the species, is not related to the concerns of a mystical system of knowledge.

Science, if one were to believe the propagandists, is said to be all-pervasive. But this claim rests on a broad and loose use of the term. Neither our political or economic relations are systematically arranged according to a formal theory of society, nor is there any such arrangement in any other nation. There is science in the United States; but it forms a distinct subculture which is dependent on other nonscientific portions of society for its resources, and its results are subsequently used by them. The prevailing system of knowledge in the modern world, the system of knowledge which typically dictates the development and use of science, is a modern form of magic.

The evidence of modern magic can be found in the continued bias against rational theory (or the reduction of the meaning of theory to empirical generalization); the trial and error methods of investigation so prevalent in political and economic enterprise and social science; the popularity of empiricist philosophy (under such names as positivism, operationalism, and existentialism); and even in the common use of empirical association for explanations as diverse as the attribution of air pollution to the automobile and the success of a politician, to a national "feeling" that we need more "law and order." Corresponding to the witch doctor is the physician with his ignorance of modern biology. Corresponding to the primitive spell is modern advertising which offers products which assure long life, happiness, and popularity through the ritual use of the most powerful detergent, the most stylish cigarette, or the strongest deodorant. Corresponding to the primitive chief is the modern chief of state, the man of power, the manipulator of nations and men, who acts in complete ignorance of any political or social theory.

Although modern magic is similar in appearance to the magic of primitives because it shares the use of empirical thought and empirical power, it is different in a number of important ways. The scope of its effects is much greater because of the longer and more extensive tradition behind it, because of its connections with the results of modern science, and because it can be more conscious and systematic. David Hume and John Stuart Mill effectively systematized empiricism in such a way that the attribution of empirical connection is now more effective in developed nations than in primitive communities. The meteorologist, although he may approach the study of the weather only through empirical association of events, will reject the Hopi rain dance as a means of producing rain simply because his more rigorous rules for empirical connection supply him with more extensive knowledge of weather throughout the world. He has studied the appearance of rain in conjunction with all sorts of other empirical phenomena, and he knows that it is more often associated with them than with dancing.

Modern magic also differs from more primitive forms in that it does not necessarily view the world as an interconnected whole. Although some empiricists may accept this view in general, it has no direct effect upon their specific actions because specific actions are connected to other empirical events only through generalization. Empirical generalization, however, results in looser connections between specific actions as more and more actions are included in its scope. Magic is an inefficient means of concentrating knowledge since as its scope of knowledge increases the difficulty of handling it increases proportionately. As soon as the concerns of man increase greatly in scope, they become too unwieldy to be accumulated in one mind. This necessarily results in a division of knowledge into independent areas having little or nothing to do with one another in their development. The parts are disconnected from the whole and develop into specializations such as those of physician, politician, radio repairman, construction worker, and typist, leading to the loss of the notion that the world is composed of systematically interrelated parts. This circumstance is particularly crucial to the development and maintenance of the problems of the modern world.

In modern magic the establishment of empirical connection is separated from the actual wielding of power in the sense that the centralized control of military, political, and economic power in the hands of an elite essentially relegates to them the exclusive positions of power-holding, while the actual responsibility of establishing empirical connection is the concern of subordinate specialists, the staff. Sciences thus are viewed as dependent but necessary specializations whose results are used rightfully only by members of the elite. If a scientist were to attempt to determine the utilization of the knowledge he or others had created, he would be no longer acting as a scientist, according to the elite viewpoint, but as a politician. In sociology this strange separation is accepted. It is claimed that it is scientific to work for the war department as long as the social scientist does not use the results for himself but hands them over to the power-holders. It is believed that it is unscientific to become active in politics for reform or revolution. In effect, then, the sociologist's idea of his science is that it is an empiricist endeavor shorn of power. If power were introduced it would no longer be a science. Fortunately, this idea of "value neutrality" is not as common in the real sciences.

To hold empirical power over a society, however, does not imply effective control of that society from a scientific point of view. Regardless of how much that empirical power is concentrated in an elite, it does not assure that any individual or group can actually control the multitudinous consequences of action in the society it dominates. Although it is evident that this empiricist power has been concentrated in the hope of controlling society, that is not necessarily the result of such concentration. This may be clearly demonstrated through Weber's explanation of the fall of Rome.[2] The economic basis of Roman civilization was the manor whose profits were based on the exploitation of slaves. Free labor had to compete with slaves, and consequently it too could be exploited. The exploitation of slaves, however, was so intensive that they either could not or would not reproduce themselves. This meant that constant expansion of the empire was necessary to capture new slaves. In order to carry out this expansion, a gigantic army was necessary. But the size of the army was dependent upon the number of slaves and the extent of their exploitation. Rome expanded until it reached its natural limits determined primarily by external barbarian pressure and the costs of transportation by land and water. Inland transportation was far more expensive, and access to rivers was thus essential to the maintenance of urban centers. Once Rome expanded beyond the water routes, costs increased prohibitively and expansion stopped. When expansion stopped, the source of slaves stopped, and the existing slaves had to be made to reproduce or the manors would cease to exist profitably. The improvement of the conditions of the slaves so that they could reproduce would have required that they be allowed to live in separate dwellings and to marry. In effect, they had is be made into serfs. The transition meant a reduction of the level of exploitation and thus profits, and finally the loss of money with which to support the army. Legions were no longer at full strength, there were fewer of them, and Rome could no longer defend her territories against the bar-

---

[2] See Max Weber, "The Social Causes of the Decay of Ancient Civilization," in *Studies in Explanation: A Reader in the Philosophy of Science* (Englewood Cliffs: Prentice-Hall, Inc., 1963), pp. 339–55.

barian invasion which further weakened the economic structure. Landowners returned to their land and built private forts to protect themselves; this led to the fall of Rome and the rise of feudalism.

During the beginning of this process, power was increasingly concentrated in the hands of the emperor, but the concentration had no effect upon the control of society itself. Rome fell, not because of the concentration of power, but in spite of it. No wonder Marx claimed that each society contains within itself the seeds of its own destruction. Rome was based on a slave system, and it was the slave system which led to its destruction. Western civilization is based on technological expansion. Is this likely to lead to the final destruction of society?

Modern technology consists of the magical application of science for empirical ends. Science exists, according to the empirical view, in order to create knowledge which can be applied as a means to the accumulation of power. Both economic enterprise and politics have consistently maintained this view throughout the history of the development of science. In the working of the technological-magical system, resources are allocated for the creation of scientific knowledge and to support some individuals who utilize a scientific system of knowledge. Their knowledge is passed on to empirically oriented technicians and engineers for application in developing new, more effective techniques for the accumulation of empirical power which, in turn, leads to more support for the technological system. The scientist is embedded in the system, and presumably his interests are those of the system itself because of the support he derives from it. The development of science has thus been associated closely with the increase of empirical power within the technological system. The control of action in this process has been empirical, with the result that sciences have developed at considerably different rates according to the apparent power which could result from their use. Astronomy was supported by the British government for improved navigation; physics was supported by the United States government to develop the nuclear bomb; chemistry has been supported by diverse industries such as rubber, petroleum, and beer for increased profits. Science for its own sake can occasionally be found, in universities for example; but the support of universities in the United States by the government and industry seems to be influencing the development of science for profit and power.

The technological utilization of science is dangerous, for the empirical power which results is far beyond that which a technological-magical system of knowledge can effectively control. The puny powers wielded by individuals in primitive magical systems were not dangerous to more than small collectivities of individuals, but the powers exercised by modern empirical thinkers could result in the destruction of life itself. As Barry Commoner has explained, "Modern science and technology are simply too powerful to permit a trial and error approach."[3] Yet, because it lacks rational theory, trial and error is the approach of empirical thinkers to the testing of knowledge. He adds, "Are we really in control of the vast new powers that science has given us or is there a danger that science is getting out of hand?"[4] He concludes rightly that we are not, and that it is. The powers generated by the selective development of modern science are simply too great for control by empirical thinkers. The oceans show the error of creating a whole industry to manufacture detergents. More than one out of ten Americans is connected with the automobile industry which has effected the increase of carbon dioxide in the atmosphere which dangerously threatens to change the world's weather. The struggle of less industrialized nations to industrialize only serves to further pollute the environment. The trial and error testing of nuclear weapons has not only led to the possibility of destroying mankind through the use of bombs but also to traces of radioactivity in the bones of every living man. Perhaps the use of these weapons in nuclear war will be the final test of whether civilization will survive. The empiricist power-holders see these weapons only as evidence of their great power, but the scientist knows that the exercise of this power would be final.

If modern science is to be used for empirical ends, as it is today, its developments must be kept secret. As in the case of the primitive magician with his spells, knowledge is power only if I have it and you don't. The result is governmental and industrial secrecy which has led to a dangerous erosion of the integrity of science. The integrity of science rests upon its self-correcting character. But science is self-correcting only when scientists act as a community, and when communication is freely permitted. The immediate result of the lack of communication is the duplication of scientific study not only within the United States but in other nations as well. Human resources are wasted as a consequence, and the realization of the importance of the interdependence of scientific knowledge is seldom recognized. As Commoner has explained, "A nuclear test explosion is usually regarded as an experiment in engineering and physics; but it is also a vast, if poorly controlled, experiment in environmental biology. It is a convincing statement of the competence of modern physics and engineering, but also a demonstration of the poor understanding of the biology of fallout."[5] To the empiricist power holder the bomb was the trial and the fallout the error to be covered up with secrecy.

Not only is empiricism unable to control science, it increasingly impedes its development. Orwell's *1984* and Huxley's *Brave New World* represent possible end points of a trend evident today. In both societies science was completely subservient to power holders. In *1984* world conflict was ritual-

---

[3] Barry Commoner, *Science and Survival* (New York: The Viking Press, 1963), p. 29.
[4] *Ibid.*, p. 8.
[5] *Ibid.*, p. 25.

ized so that science could be eliminated, for its inherent freedom of thought posed a threat to the ruling class.

Science has been empirically subordinated within the technological system, but this has not led to control of its effects, for empiricism is too simplistic in structure to handle the complex developments of science. Modern magic does not work *for* people but *against* them. Nor can religion or religious moral systems of knowledge control the results of science. As Commoner has pointed out, the problems of the modern world cannot be "perceived in terms of the casting of stones or the theft of a neighbor's ox."[6] It is not that scientists should take a moral stand, for scientists are relatively powerless within the system and do not control the news media or the government. Even if they could inform the public, the confused and powerless public does not have the means to solve the world's problems. Science is not only a dependent subculture unable to influence action, but the division of science itself into specialties precludes its rational use. In a recent editorial in *Science*, the official voice of the American Association for the Advancement of Science, Amitai Etzioni dismissed the concern with the pollution of the environment as a "fad."[7] He claimed that "Fighting hunger, malnutrition, and rats should be given priority over saving wildlife, and improving our schools over constructing waste disposal systems. If we must turn to 'environment' first attention should be given to the 57,000 Americans who will *lose their lives* on the roads in 1970."[8] This statement is unfortunately typical of the parochial attitude of social scientists. It displays an appalling ignorance of the interconnectedness of society and the environment and a determined narrowness in relation to the importance of integrating scientific knowledge. It is empirically rooted in the concerns of the immediate present without rational calculation of any sort that might lead to a program for ensuring life in the future. Yet it takes very little imagination to see that both poverty and pollution have a common origin in the technological-magical power system and that the conditions for the elimination of one are the conditions for the elimination of the other.

Modern empiricism is no more in control of society than were the Roman emperors. The mere concentration of power cannot solve the problem of control if the sciences are segmented. The empirical power of Western civilization is increasingly concentrated in the elite of the United States, but this monopoly of empirical power is insufficient to control the course of society based on the expansion of technology. Mental and manual laborers are manipulated by that power, but the combined results of their actions are neither understood nor controlled. Instead of slaves, capital and profits

---

[6] *Ibid.*, p. 130.

[7] Amitai Etzioni, "The Wrong Top Priority," *Science*, 168 (May 22, 1970), 921.

[8] *Ibid.*, p. 921.

form the basis of power. But capital costs do not include poverty and racism or pollution in their calculations. All three must be continued if power concentration is to continue. It is evident, however, that if present conditions continue the system will fall. If it does not fall through nuclear war or revolution, it will pollute itself and the rest of civilization out of existence. These are necessary outcomes of the empiricist guided technological system.

The hope has been raised that a solution to these problems can be found in a new humanism which would transform the goals of the dominant technological-magical system of knowledge. After all, primitive magic is personal, and in a sense humanistic, but modern magic is impersonal and not at all humanistic in orientation. Marx and Engels explained this impersonality as a consequence of the inability of modern man to control the forces of his society. His impersonality was a reflection of the seemingly impersonal forces which controlled him. Weber explained the same phenomena similarly and added that base materialism is a necessary condition for its continuation, a materialism ever more evident with the fall of religion. This would result in "Specialists without spirit, sensualists without heart; this nullity imagines that it has attained a level of civilization never before achieved."[9] Machine production and its relations determine the lives of those born into the structure. Would this continue, Weber asked, "until the last ton of fossilized coal is burnt?"[10]

The dehumanization of modern society is furthered by bureaucratization. Bureaucracies are constructed to concentrate empirical power, but in the process the powers of individuals in the structure must be nullified. Impersonality of rules and relations is the means to that end. Today the legal structure, even in democracies, shows similar effects in its threats of impersonal violence. Punishment is not personal in terms of "an eye for an eye" but is relegated in terms of an impersonal structure of "law and order."

Empiricism is personal in primitive societies, for it takes place in the context of simple face to face relations between members of a small group. In those conditions individuals can be treated as individuals. In a complex technological structure, however, empirical attempts to maintain control over widely divided and specialized groups can only take place through generalization. Thus instead of relating individual to individual, each person is considered only as a member of a group (a doctor, a Negro, a member of the working class, a physicist, etc.), a part of a generalized category. To be treated as a part of a generalized category is to be treated impersonally, and the result is dehumanization. A head of state, a president, or a governor who would never with his own hands kill another human being thus can

---

[9] Max Weber, *The Protestant Ethic and the Spirit of Capitalism*, trans. Talcott Parsons (New York: Charles Scribner's Sons, 1958), p. 182.

[10] *Ibid.*, p. 181.

disclaim responsibility for the killing of so many Viet Cong, blacks, and students under the safe cover of impersonality. These are not thought of personally as people but as members of general categories and are moreover a threat to the continued existence of empirical power.

Clearly only a scientific system of knowledge can effectively control the diverse results of science. Certain conditions must be met in order to bring the scattered results of divided science under the control of a scientific system of knowledge. As Commoner has pointed out, "The separation of the laws of nature among different sciences is a human conceit; nature itself is an integrated whole."[11] The notion of the interdependence of natural phenomena found in primitive magical knowledge is lost in the impersonality of modern magic because of the inability of empirical generalization to deal with complex society. Science, however, does not suffer from that weakness, for its rationalization into a formally consistent system is a continuing process in spite of its complexity. Science as a whole can be self-correcting only to the extent that rationalization is complete; this requires the free flow of information to counteract the unbalanced development of specific sciences according to their apparent differential utility as a means to empirical power. Commoner argues that if biological science were further developed and rationalized with physics, the empirical blunders which led to fallout would not have taken place.

Commoner's basic idea is correct, but the scope of his solution is too narrow. The integration of biology and physics is not sufficient if they are still subordinated to political and economic powers, for the ends of these powers are neither scientific nor grounded in the goal of providing support for life. The development of a scientific system of knowledge to control the results of science requires the balanced development of all sciences, especially social science which has lagged dangerously behind. Science cannot hope to be self-correcting in the absence of social science.

The development of social science is doubly important, for it is from the social area in economics and politics that empiricist power controls the other sciences. The maintenance of empiricist power is dependent upon the maintenance of the technological-magical system of knowledge. The development of scientific social science should lead to the end of the empiricist power system and its technological base because science leads to the downfall of empiricism through its scope of explanation and resulting efficiency.

But the so-called social scientist owes his support to the technological-magical system, and instead of transcending it he seems limited by it. Graduate students are required to do "empirical studies," and such studies receive *all* of the federal, foundation, and commercial support as well as space in the professional journals. Rationality is systematically excluded from the

[11] Commoner, *Science and Survival*, p. 25.

study of society; nevertheless, in their ignorance of other fields, individuals within this magical system sincerely believe that they are making a contribution to science and, strangely enough, that their work is guided by theory.

There is a significant body of knowledge known as "political theory" which is subscribed to by "political scientists." But this so-called theory is no more than simple empirical generalization. It does not connect concept to concept at the theoretic level but instead states supposed empirical uniformities. The following example is typical of the empirical thinking pervasive in political science:

> Several generalizations, relating to sectional versus class conflict, the effect of candidate appeal, and the relationship of issues to turnout, are suggested by these data. The most striking feature of the over-all picture is the persistent decline in the proportion of eligible voters making use of the franchise from 1896 to 1924. This trend appears to be independent of the periodic fluctuations in turnout from one election to the next, or at least seems to result from different causes. The plateau of participation from 1876 to 1896 was, in the first place, sustained by the sectional tensions associated with the Civil War, when the bloody shirt was flourished frequently as the symbol of the great conflict between North and South. ... some alleviation of economic discontent and a growth of commercial centers reduced the tendency of the West to make the sectional struggle the center of politics. With the parties presenting less sharp choices of policies, say Schlesinger and Eriksson, voter interest dropped off.[12]

The author of this believes that he has explained a political occurrence; however, his explanation certainly is not scientific since it lacks both concepts and rational connection. The statement consists of no more than a broad generalization, and the claimed explanation is no more than a set of sub-generalizations. This is no more than an empirical-magical association of events.

Political sociology is no more scientific:

> The findings of public opinion surveys in thirteen different counties that the lower strata are less committed to democratic norms than the middle classes are reaffirmed by the research of more psychologically oriented investigators, who have studied the social correlates of the "authoritarian personality." Many studies in this area, summarized recently, show a consistent association between authoritarianism and lower-class status. One survey of 460 Los Angeles adults reported that "the working class contains a higher proportion of authoritarians than either the middle or upper class," and that among workers, those who explicitly identified themselves as "working class" rather than "middle class" were more authoritarian.[13]

---

[12] Robert E. Lane, *Political Life: Why and How People Get Involved in Politics* (New York: The Free Press, 1959), p. 23.

[13] Seymour Martin Lipset, *Political Man: The Social Bases of Politics* (Garden City: Doubleday & Company, 1963), pp. 95–96.

From these and other selected studies the author makes the empirical generalization that "the poorer are more intolerant."[14] Again an empirical-magical explanation. Empirical events are explained by empirical events. The associations made here are no more theoretically valid than the associations made by primitives which the modern Westerner would view with scorn as superstition or false knowledge. Empirical connection isolated from concepts and theoretic connections is the basis of explanation.

Most of economic "theory" is likewise empirical; but micro-economic theory is actually theoretic, using concepts such as ideal market, price, supply, and demand in such a way that necessary consequences can be drawn from their relationships with one another. This theory, however, is only useful for the rare empirical conditions approximating an ideal market. No comprehensive theory has been developed to cover other types of markets, and in these cases economic interpretation has been a matter of empirical generalization. And even micro-economics is not a dynamic theory with which predictions can be made for long time periods or in relation to the economics of the technological-magical system. Instead we are offered the "trend analysis of experts" which is simply empirical guessing. Most of the problems of national economic policy transcend the limits of the scientific portion of economics, and it is precisely in this area that economic empirical thinking seems to correspond with the interests of the economically successful, those who hold magical power.

The anthropologist too, whatever his claim, is typically an empirical thinker utilizing a magical system of knowledge just like his more primitive subjects. His goal is a simple empirical one—description; and his attempts to understand native thought are not related to theory but simply strive for more accurate description. He recognizes that, from his own point of view, he may never fully understand the ideas of another culture and often writes treatises on how to best describe the native. There is, indeed, a relatively new school in anthropology, that of "structural" anthropology, which claims to view native thought rationally. But structural anthropology is unfortunately just as empirical-magical as descriptive anthropology. Instead of viewing native cultures from the point of view of concepts in a rationally connected system, it views them in terms of simple empirical categories such as opposites. Classifying elements of native cultures in terms of observed opposites is a simple empirical procedure—it merely describes those elements according to perceived external characteristics. It does not go beyond description to theoretical explanation.

Sociology also claims to be scientific but, like anthropology, it lacks theory. Sociologists tend to divide themselves into two camps: the "methodologists" and "researchers," and the "theorists." The implication is that the

[14] *Ibid.*, p. 92.

former group devotes itself to techniques of scientific measurement and research while the latter is concerned with the development and study of theory. Of course, as long as the two endeavors remain separate, they are not scientific. Even then, an examination of sociological work leads to the definite conclusion that it is neither concerned with measurement nor theory, but only with two types of empirical thinking.

"Methodology" tends to be concerned with the problem of placing observed phenomena in empirical categories represented by numbers. This procedure is not a means of interpreting a theoretic calculus but is merely a process of putting numerical tags on particular empirical observations. The results of such operations are particular sets of figures which cannot be used for comparison of circumstances, let alone rational calculation.

"Theory" on the other hand is a label given to broad empirical generalizations about social phenomena. These generalizations are intended to point out the natural regularities of society, ignoring the fact that theories and laws are not "discovered" in nature and do not consist of generalization. One group of such theorists are the "functionalists" who are concerned with pointing out the functions of particular social phenomena. This, of course, is a descriptive task simply involving the isolation of social functions of elements of "social systems." To describe an object's function is merely to point out what is does or what its position is, to make a descriptive generalization about the object in terms of a particular type of observed characteristic.

The technological-magical political and economic structure supports and encourages scientific research and study in physical and chemical areas because the results of such work can be used for centralization and accumulation of wealth and power. The development of contraceptive pills or new food additives is profitable to the individual who markets them and leads to accumulated economic power. The possible harmful effects of these developments on the relatively powerless and ignorant individuals who use such products are ignored both by the manufacturers and their political structure in their search for power. Political and economic power are in this sense inseparable—both participate in the accumulation of magical power. Political action may be taken to remove harmful products from the market, but this action is usually taken only after the products have lost their profit making potential when the public has belatedly been informed of their effects.

It is not surprising therefore that those involved with political and economic power, especially in the United States and the Soviet Union, do not support scientific study of society, for such work would clearly point out that their actions do not support humanity. Empirical studies trying to discover the proportion of opinions on certain objects, individual values, likes and dislikes, club membership, etc., do not lead to criticism of political or economic policy and are occasionally useful in the accumulation of power. The role of the social scientist is often reduced to the equivalent of a spy in the reporting of such information. But theoretical work is not supported.

Man's scientific knowledge, although great in some areas, is essentially nil in others because of the lack of support for scientific work which does not contribute to the accumulation of empirical power. The complex problems of the world can no longer be solved by magical, mystical, or religious systems of knowledge. Only an integrated science is capable of controlling the vast problems created by the empirical use of science for profit and power. Only integrated science can turn us from the petty concerns of controlling men to controlling our physical and social conditions for the survival of men. Only integrated science is capable at this late date of producing the knowledge necessary to turn men away from their present course of self-destruction.

INDEX